W9-CIB-684

Hi, I'm Harry.

I came up with this directory for my dad and I to know everywhere to go in New York City that is Paw Friendly.

Now we're sharing it with you.

I hope that this book will help you and your four legged children to enjoy New York City as much as it has helped us.

I would like to give special thanks to:

Farrel Green for conceiving and directing this concept
Matt Kirschner for design and layout
Roi Werner for cover and additional design
And you for purchasing, using and supporting this book

First edition copywrite July, 2001

You can email me for more info at:
harry@pawfriendlyguide.com

i

HARRY'S

Paw Friendly Guide

NEIGHBORHOODS

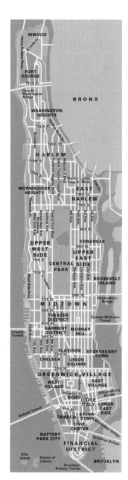

HARRY'S

Paw Friendly Guide

CATEGORIES

* Outdoor cafes only

In loving memory of
Harry's Grandmother
Melanie

Neighborhood Listings
By Category

Parks

Alice in Wonderland
E. 74th St.
North of Conservatory Water

Belvedere Castle
Mid-Park (79th/80th)
11am - 4pm Wed - Mon

Bethesda Terrace
Mid-Park (@ 72nd St.)

Carousel
Mid-Park (@ 64th St.)

Dog Hill (Cedar Hill)
East-Side Park (76th-79th)

George Delacorte Musical Clock
East-Side Park (63rd-66th)

The Great Hill
West-Side Park (103rd-107th)

Harlem Meer Loch
West-Side Park (100th-103rd)

Loeb Boat House & Lake
Boat House - East
(74th/75th)
Lake - Mid-Park (71st-78th)

Parks (cont'd)

Model Boat Pond, Conservatory Water
East-Side (72nd-75th)

The Ramble
Mid-Park (73rd-79th)

Ravine
Mid-Park (102nd-106th)

Reservoir
Mid-Park (85th-96th)

Scholars Walk
East-Side (@ 59th St.)

Shakespeare Garden
Mid-Park (@ 79th St.)

Strawberry Fields
72nd St & Central Park West

Zoo
East-Side (@ 59th)

Dog Runs

Chelsea Waterside Park
22nd St.
(11th Ave./West Side Hwy)

Hudson Esplanade Walk
Between Chelsea Piers &
Battery Park.

Gifts

La Maison Moderne
144 W. 19th St. (6th/7th)

Home Furnishings

Bed, Bath & Beyond
6th Ave. (@ 17th St.)

La Maison Moderne
144 W. 19th St. (6th/7th)

Home Furnishings (cont'd)

New York Home
37 W. 17th St.
212.366.6880

Kid's

Chelsea Kids Quarters
33 W. 17th St. (5th/6th)
212.627.5524

Men's Accessories

Lambertson Truex.com
19 W. 21st St.
212.243.7671
www.lambertsontruex.com

Men's Clothes

Gerry's Menswear
110 8th Ave.
212.243.9141

Pet Supls/Svcs

Andrea Arden Dog Training
212.213.4288

Bonnie's K9 Corp.
136 9th Ave.
212.414.2500
www.k9-swimtherapy.copy

City Dogs Obedience School
158 W. 23rd St. (6th/7th)
212.255.3618

Heart of Chelsea Animal Hospital
257 W. 18th St.
212.924.6116

Pet Supls/Svcs (cont'd)

New York Dog Spa & Hotel
145 W. 18th St. (6th/7th)
212.243.1199

Pet Parade LTD., The
144 W. 19th St.
212.645.5345
www.thepetparadeltd.com

Real Estate

Fenwick-Keats Downtown, LLC
201 W. 11th St.
212.352.8144

Restaurants
(outdoor only)

Cafeteria
119 7th Ave. (@ 17t St.)
212.414.1717

Restaurants (cont'd)

Chelsea Grill
135 8th Ave. (16th/17th)
212.255.3618

Chelsea Lobster Company
156 7th Ave. (@ 19th St.)
212.243.5732

Le Singe Vert
160 7th Ave. (19th/20th)
212.366.4100

Merchant's
112 7th Ave.

Paul & Jimmy's Ristorante
123 E. 18th St.
212.475.9540

Petite Abeille
107 W. 18th St. (6th/7th)
212.604.9350

Raymond's Cafe
88 7th Ave. (15th/16th)
212.929.1778

Restaurants (cont'd)

Restivo Ristorante
209 7th Ave. (@ 22nd St.)
212.366.4133

Shoes

Man's Fashionable Shoes
196 1/2 7th Ave. (21st/22nd)
212.675.0718

Medici
24 W. 23rd St. (5th/6th)
212.604.0888
mediciinc@msn.com

Sacco
94 7th Ave. (@ 16th)
212.675.5180
www.saccoshoes.com

Women's Accessories

Lambertson Truex.com
19 W. 21st St.
212.243.7671
www.lambertsontruex.com

Misc.

A.I. Friedman
44 W. 18th St.
212.243.9000
www.aifriedman.com

Cleaners

Fancy Cleaners & Tailors
384 3rd Ave.
212.481.1112

Fancy Cleaners & Tailors
1087 2nd Ave.
212.223.7455

Fancy Cleaners & Tailors
254 3rd Ave.
212.982.2007

Fancy Cleaners & Tailors
860-870 UN Plaza Vale
212.759.2006

Copy & Printing Svcs.

Tower Copy
427 3rd Ave.
212.679.3509
www.inch.com/~tce

Cosmetics

Aveda
509 Madison Ave
212.832.2416

Sephora
212.245.1633

Qiora
535 Madison Ave
212.527.9933

Dog Runs

Peter Detmold Park
Beekman Pl
(49th - 51st @ FDR Drive)

Robert Moses Park
42nd St. (1st Ave/FDR Drive)

Madison Square Park
25th St. (@ Madison Ave.)

Eyewear

Cohen's
108 E. 23rd St.
212.677.3707

Eyewear (cont'd)

Elite Optique
510 Madison Ave
212.421.1164

Gramercy Eyewear
240 3rd Ave
212.254.5535

H.L. Purdy, Inc.
501 Madison Ave
212.688.8050
sales@hlpurdy.com
www.hlpurdy.com

Qiora
535 Madison Ave
212.527.9933

Selima @ Barneys NY
600 Madison Ave.
212.833.2038

Gifts

Body Shop, The
509 Madison Ave
212.829.8603

Gifts (cont'd)

Body Shop, The
Rockefeller Center

Body Shop, The
41st St. (@ 5th Ave.)

Crabtree & Evelyn, LTD.
520 Madison Ave
212.758.7847
www.crabtree-evelyn.com

Hides In Shape
555 Madison Ave
212.371.5998

Hides In Shape
630 3rd Ave.
212.661.2590

Paper Emporium
835A 2nd Ave
212.697.6573

Rebecca Moss, LTD
510 Madison Ave
212.832.7671

Staghorn, LTD
362 3rd Ave. (@ 26th St.)
212.832.2416

Home Furnishings

Kama
368 3rd Ave.
212.689.7517

Staghorn, LTD
362 3rd Ave. (@ 26th St.)
212.832.2416

Simon's Hardware & Bath
421 3rd Ave.
212.532.9220

Hotels

Four Seasons, The
57 E. 57th St.
www.fourseasons.com

Loews Hotel
569 Lexington Ave.
212.752.7000

Roger Williams, The
44 W. 44th St.
212.448.7000

Hotels (cont'd)

Royalton Hotel
368 3rd Ave.
212.869.4400

St. Regis Hotel
2 E. 55th St.
212.753.4500

Jewelry

Cellini, NYC
509 Madison Ave.(@ 53rd St.)
212.888.0505

Links
535 Madison Ave.
212.588.1177
800.210.0079

Staghorn, LTD
362 3rd Ave. (@ 26th St.)
212.832.2416

Tiffany & Co.
725 5th Ave (@57th)

Liquor Stores

D'vine Wines & Spirits
764 3rd Ave. (47th/48th)
212.317.1169

Thomas J. McAdam Liquor Co., Inc.
308 3rd Ave.
212.683.3276
212.679.1224/5
www.mcadam-buyrite.com

Men's Accessories

Asprey & Garrard
725 5th Ave. (@ 56th St.)
212.688.1811

Body Shop, The
509 Madison Ave
212.829.8603

Body Shop, The
Rockefeller Center

Body Shop, The
41st St. (@ 5th Ave.)

Men's Accessories (cont'd)

Hides In Shape
555 Madison Ave
212.371.5998

Hides In Shape
630 3rd Ave.
212.661.2590

Kama
368 3rd Ave.
212.689.7517

Links
535 Madison Ave.
212.588.1177
800.210.0079

Prada
750 5th Ave. (56th/57th)
212.664.0010

Tumi
520 Madison Ave. (@ 54th)
212.813.0545

Men's Clothes

Club Monaco
55th St. (@ 5th Ave)
646.497.1116

H. Herzfeld, Inc.
507 Madison Ave
212.753.6756
www.herzfeldonline.com

Kama
368 3rd Ave.
212.689.7517

Prada
750 5th Ave. (56th/57th)
212.664.0010

Saks 5th Ave.
611 5th Ave. (@ 50th)
212.753.4000

Vintage Thrift Shop, The
286 3rd Ave. (22nd/23rd)
212.871.0777

Parks

St. Vartan's Park
1st Ave. (35th -36th)

Parks (cont'd)

Sutton Place Park
Sutton Place S. (54th - 57th)

Pet Supls/Svcs

Andrea Arden Dog Training
212.213.4288

Biscuits & Bath
227 E. 44th St.
212.692.2324

Doggie Do (and Pussycats Too!)
567 3rd Ave (37th/38th)
212.661.9111

Natural Pet, The
238 3rd Ave.
212.228.4848

Prada
750 5th Ave. (56th/57th)
212.664.0010

Pet Supls/Svcs (cont'd)

Saks 5th Ave.
611 5th Ave. (@ 50th)
212.753.4000

Two Dogs & A Goat!
326 E. 34th St.
212.213.6979

Restaurants (outdoor only)

Cafe De Paris
924 2nd Ave. (@ 49th St.)
212.486.1411

Cafe St. Bart's
109 E. 50th St. (@ Park)
212.888.2664

Christina's
606 2nd Ave. (33rd/34th)
212.889.5169

Cinema
2 E. 45th St.
212.949.0600
www.cinemarestaurants.com

Restaurants (cont'd)

Cinema
505 3rd Ave.
212.689.9022
www.cinemarestaurants.com

Friend Of A Farmer
77 Irving Pl.
212.477.2188

San Pietro
18 E. 54th St.
212.753.9015
www.sanpietro.net

Typhoon
22 E. 54th St.
212.754.9006

Shoes

Fratelli Rossetti
625 Madison Ave.
212.888.5107

Johnston & Murphy
345 Madison Ave.

Shoes (cont'd)

Johnston & Murphy
520 Madison Ave.

Maraolo
782 Lexington Ave.
212.832.8182

Maraolo
551 Madison Ave.
212.308.8794

Maraolo
835 Madison Ave.
212.628.5080

Telephone Supls/Svcs

Mobile City
575 5th Ave.

Mobile City
575 Madison Ave.

Personal Communication Center
220 3rd Ave.
212.253.0800

Telephone Supls/Svcs (cont'd)

Wireless Concepts
489 3rd Ave.
212.679.6077
msrlinks@aol.com

Women's Accessories

Body Shop, The
509 Madison Ave
212.829.8603

Body Shop, The
Rockefeller Center

Body Shop, The
41st St. (@ 5th Ave.)

Hides In Shape
555 Madison Ave
212.371.5998

Hides In Shape
630 3rd Ave.
212.661.2590

Women's Accessories (cont'd)

Kama
368 3rd Ave.
212.689.7517

Links
535 Madison Ave.
212.588.1177
800.210.0079

Michel's Bags
672 Lexington Ave(55th/56th)
212.872.1320

Michel's Bags
510 Madison Ave.(52nd/53rd)
212.355.8309

Prada
750 5th Ave. (56th/57th)
212.664.0010

Tumi
520 Madison Ave. (@ 54th)
212.813.0545

Zan Boutique
810 2nd Ave. (@ 43rd St.)
212.687.3304

Women's Clothes

Club Monaco
55th St. (@ 5th Ave)
646.497.1116

Eileen Fisher
521 Madison Ave.
212.759.9888

Fogal
510 Madison Ave.
info@fogal.com

Kama
368 3rd Ave.
212.689.7517

Prada
750 5th Ave. (56th/57th)
212.664.0010

Saks 5th Ave.
611 5th Ave. (@ 50th)
212.753.4000

Vintage Thrift Shop, The
286 3rd Ave. (22nd/23rd)
212.871.0777

Zan Boutique
810 2nd Ave. (@ 43rd St.)
212.687.3304

Misc.

Davidoff
535 Madison Ave
212.751.9060
800.548.4623

Paper Emporium
835A 2nd Ave
212.697.6573

Rebecca Moss, LTD
510 Madison Ave
212.832.7671

Scully & Scully Park Ave.
504 Park Ave. (@59th)
800.223.3717

Cleaners

Fancy Cleaners & Tailors
176 2nd Ave.
212.677.7757

Fancy Cleaners & Tailors
40 E. 8th St.
212.358.1133

Kim's Cleaners
99 Ave. A
212.260.0697

Young's Cleaners
17th St. (@ 3rd Ave.)
212.473.6154

Dog Runs

Fish Bridge Park
Dover St.
(Pearl/Water off Bklyn Bridge)

Tompkins Square Park
1st Ave. & Ave. B (7th-10th)

Dog Runs (cont'd)

Stuyvesant Park Ball Fields
6th-12th St and FDR Drive

Eyewear

Selima Optique
84 E. 7th St.
212.260.2495

Myoptics
42 St. Mark's Pl.
212.533.1577

Gifts

Body Shop, The
8th St. (@ Broadway)

Exit 9
64 Ave. A
212.228.0145

Home Furnishings

Exit 9
64 Ave. A
212.228.0145

Galleria J. Antonio
47 Ave. A
212.505.5512

Jewelry

Galleria J. Antonio
47 Ave. A
212.505.5512

The Shape of Lies
127 E. 7th St.
212.533.5420

Kid's

Joanie James
117 E. 7th St.
212.505.9653

Men's Accessories

Body Shop, The
8th St. (@ Broadway)

Men's Clothes

Garosparo
119 St. Mark's Pl.
(1st/Ave. A)
212.533.7835

Music

Etherea
66 Ave. A
212.358.1126

Kim's Video & Music
6 St. Mark's Pl.
212.598.9985

Parks

Avenue B Art Garden
6th St and Ave. B

Chrystie Garden, The
Houston St. (1st - 2nd Ave.)

East River Walk
12th - Montgomery
(FDR/East River)

Stuyvesant Park
15th - 17th St. (2nd/3rd)

Tompkins Square Park
1st Ave - Ave B and
7th - 10th St.

Pet Supls/Svcs

Animal Crackers
26 1st Ave.
212.614.6786

Mikey's Pet Shop, Inc.
130 E 7th St.
212.477.3235

Photographic Services

Good Impression
214 3rd Ave.
212.539.0903

Restaurants
(Outdoor Only)

Aunt B's on B
186 Ave. B. (11th/12th)
212.505.2071

Black-Eyed Suzie's Organic
128 E 7th St. (1st/Ave. A)
212.388.0707

Cafe Margaux
175 Ave. B (@ 11th St.)
212.260.7960

Casimir
103 Ave. B. (6th/7th)
212.995.5991

Crooked Tree Creperie
110 St. Mark's Pl.
(1st/Ave. A)
212.533.3299

Restaurants (cont'd)

Life Cafe
343 E. 10th St. (off Ave. B)
212.477.8791
www.lifecafenyc.com

La Gould Finch
93 Ave. B (@ 6th St.)
212.253.6369

Mesapotamia
98 Ave. B. (6th/7th)
212.358.1166

Ovo
65 2nd Ave. (3rd/4th)
212.353.1444

Pierrot Bistro
28 Ave. B (2nd/3rd)
212.673.1999

Pisces
95 Ave. A (@ 6th St.)
212.260.6660

Telephone Bar & Grill
149 2nd Ave. (9th/10th)
212.529.5000

Shoes

Profiles
30 3rd Ave.
212.979.9724
siriam@webtv.net

Video

Kim's Video & Music
6 St. Mark's Pl.
212.505.0311

Women's Accessories

Body Shop, The
8th St. (@ Broadway)

Women's Clothes

Cherry Bishop Clothing
117-119 E. 7th St.
212.529.4608

Garosparo
119 St. Mark's Pl.
(1st/Ave. A)
212.533.7835

Mode
109 St. Mark's Pl.
212.529.9208

Mo Mo Fa Lana
43 Ave. A
212.979.9595

Patricia Adams
115 St. Mark's Pl.
212.420.0077

Misc.

Downtown Yarn
45 Ave. A
212.995.5991

Cosmetics

Aveda
140 5th Ave.
212.645.4797

Sephora
212.674.3570

Gifts

Aveda
140 5th Ave.
212.645.4797

Body Shop, The
20th St. (@ 5th Ave.)

Men's Accessories

Body Shop, The
20th St. (@ 5th Ave.)

Men's Clothes

Club Monaco
21st St. (@ 5th Ave.)
212.352.0936

Restaurants
(Outdoor Only)

Dano Restaurant & Bar
254 5th Ave. (27th/28th)
212.725.2922

Shoes

Medici
309 5th Ave. (@ 32nd St.)
212.725.8798

Women's Accessories

Body Shop, The
20th St. (@ 5th Ave.)

Women's Clothes

Club Monaco
21st St. (@ 5th Ave.)
212.352.0936

Misc.

Typogram
318 W. 39th St.
212.736.3686

Eyewear

Selima Showroom
450 W. 15th St., Suite 650
212.206.8913

Men's Clothes

Nylon Squid
222 Lafayette St.
212.334.6554

Women's Clothes

Nylon Squid
222 Lafayette St.
212.334.6554

Eyewear

Lunettes et Chocolat
25 Prince St.
212.334.8484
212.925.8800

Gifts

Gates of Morocco, Inc.
8 Prince St.
212.925.2650

George Smith
73 Spring St.
212.226.4747

Kar'iter
19 Prince St.
212.274.1966

Lunettes et Chocolat
25 Prince St.
212.334.8484
212.925.8800

New York Firefighter's Friend
263 Lafayette St.
212.226.3142

Home Furnishings

Gates of Morocco, Inc.
8 Prince St.
212.925.2650

Kar'iter
19 Prince St.
212.274.1966

Modern Furniture Basement
132 Crosby St.
212.334.9757

Rustika
63 Crosby St.
212.965.0004

Jewelry

Dalidada
35 Spring St.
212.431.3285

Men's Clothes

Inhumane Shop
195 Mulberry St.
212.331.0499

Ina Men
262 Mott St.
212.334.2210

Minlee
7 Prince St.
212.334.6978

Nylon Squid
222 Lafayette St.
212.334.6554

X-Large
267 Lafayette St.
212.334.4480

Salons

Enve Salon
109 Crosby St.
212.334.3683

Shoes

Shoe
197 Mulberry St.
212.941.0205

Sigerson Morrison
28 Prince St.
212.219.3893

Women's Accessories

ASP
185 Mulberry St.
212.431.1682

Women's Clothes

Asp
185 Mulberry St.
646.621.3524

Baby Blue Line
238 Mott St.
212.226.5866

Women's Clothes (cont'd)

Christine Ganeaux
45 Crosby St.
212.431.4462

Claire Blaydon
202A Mott St.
212.219.1490

Inhumane Shop
195 Mulberry St.
212.331.0499

Kinnu
43 Spring St.
212.334.4775

Minlee
7 Prince St.
212.334.6978

Only Hearts
230 Mott St.
212.431.3694

Product
219 Mott St.
212.219.2224

Women's Clothes (cont'd)

Red Wong
181 Mulberry St.
212.625.1638

X-Large
267 Lafayette St.
212.334.4480

Misc.

French General
35 Crosby St.
(Broome/Grand)
212.343.7474

Animal Hospitals

TriBeCa SoHo Animal Hospital
5 Lispenard
St(Church/W.Bwy)
212.925.6100

Antiques

AIX
462 Broome St.
212.941.7919

Alice's Antiques
72 Greene St.

Paterae
458 Broome St.
212.941.0880

Aromatherapy

Illuminations
54 Spring St.
212.226.8713

Cigars

OK Cigars
383A W. Broadway
212.965.9065

Cosmetics

Aveda
233 Spring St.
212.807.1490

Aveda
456 W. Broadway
212.473.0280

Creed
9 Bond St.

Face Stockholm
110 Prince St.
212.966.9110

MAC
212.334.4641

Max Studio
415 W. Broadway
212.941.1141
www.maxstudio.com

Cosmetics (cont'd)

Sephora
212.625.1309

Shiseido Cosmetics, Ltd.
98 Prince St.
212.925.7880

Eyewear

Bond 07 by Selima
7 Bond St.
212.677.8487

Facial Index
104 Grand St.
646.613.1055

Le Corset by Selima
80 Thompson St.
212.334.4936

Morganthal Fredrics
399 W. Broadway (@ Spring)
212.966.0099

Myoptics
123 Prince St.

212.598.9306

Eyewear (cont'd)

Niwaka
464 Broome St.
212.941.5410
www.niwaka.com

Selima Optique SoHo
59 Wooster St.
212.343.9490

Galleries

Belenky Brothers
151 Wooster St.
212.674.4242

Gallery 91
91 Grand St.
212.966.3722

Oprea Gallery
115 Spring St.
212.966.6675

Ward-Nasse Gallery
178 Prince St.
212.925.6951
www.wardnasse.org

Gifts

Aveda
233 Spring St.
212.807.1490

Aveda
456 W. Broadway
212.473.0280

Chimera
77 Mercer St.
212.334.4730

Framed on Prince
124 Prince St.
212.219.9040

Julian & Sara
103 Mercer St.
212.226.1989

Prince & Sullivan 1 Hr Photo
186 Prince St.
212.941.0833

Quinto Sol
250 Lafayette St.
212.334.2255

Home Furnishings

Ad Hoc
136 Wooster St.
212.982.7703

Alice's Antiques
72 Greene St.

B Modern
153 Wooster St.
212.253.0111

Boca Grande
66 Greene St.
212.334.6120

Boffi SoHo
31 Greene St.
212.431.8282

Broadway Pan Handler
477 Broome St.

Coconut Company
131 Greene St.
212.539.1935

Craft Caravan Inc.
63 Greene St.
212.431.6669

Home Furnishings (cont'd)

Desiron
111 Greene St.
212.966.0404

Format
50 Wooster St.
212.941.7995
www.formatnyc.com

Jonathan Adler
465 Broome St.

King's Road
42 Wooster
St(Grand/Broome)
212.941.5011
www.kingsroad.com

Paterae
458 Broome St.
212.941.0880

Portico
72 Spring St.
212.941.7800
www.porticohome.com

Home Furnishings (cont'd)

Quinto Sol
250 Lafayette St.
212.334.2255

Rabun & Claiborne
115 Crosby St.
212.226.5053

Roots
270 Lafayette St., Suite 1410
212.324.3333
www.roots.com

Rustika
63 Crosby St.
212.965.0004

Sarajo
130 Greene St.
212.966.6156

Spazonavigl
113 Mercer St.
212.226.2364

Troy
138 Greene St.
212.941.4777

Home Furnishings (cont'd)

Val Cucine
152 Wooster St.
212.253.5969
www.valcucineny.com

Water Works
469 Broome St.
212.966.0605

Hotels

SoHo Grand Hotel
310 W. Broadway
800.965.3000

The Mercer
147 Mercer St.
212.966.6060

Jewelry

Belenky Brothers
151 Wooster St.
212.674.4242

Jewelry (cont'd)

Fragments
107 Greene St.
212.334.9588

Hanskoch
174 Prince St.
212.226.5385

Jack Spade
56 Greene St.
212.625.1820

Jill Platner
113 Crosby St.
212.324.1298
www.jillplatner.com

Niwaka
464 Broome St.
212.941.5410
www.niwaka.com

SoHo Gem
367 W. Broadway
212.625.3004

Stuart Moore
128 Prince St.
212.941.1023

Jewelry (cont'd)

Swatch
438 W. Broadway
646.613.0160

The Joan Michlin Gallery
56 Greene St.
212.625.1820

Versani
152 Mercer St.
212.941.7770

Yvone Christa
107 Mercer St.
212.965.1001

Kid's

Julian & Sara
103 Mercer St.
212.226.1989

Just For Tykes
83 Mercer St.
212.274.9121

Kid's (cont'd)

Lilliput
240 Lafayette St.
212.965.9567
www.lilliputsoho.com

Men's Accessories

Alexia Crawford Accessories
199 Prince St.
212.473.9703

If
94 Grand St.
212.334.4964

Jill Stuart
100 Greene St.
212.343.2300

Jack Spade
56 Greene St.
212.625.1820

Monsac
339 Broadway
212.925.3237
www.monsac.com

Men's Accessories (cont'd)

Pastel
459 Broome St.
212.219.3922

Men's Clothes

Afterlife
59 Greene St.
212.625.3167

A.P.C.
131 Mercer St.
212.966.9685

Club Monaco
Prince St.
646.533.8930

Helmut Lange
80 Greene St.
212.925.7214

Hugo Boss
132 Greene St.
212.965.1300

Men's Clothes (cont'd)

John Varuatos
149 Mercer St.
212.965.0700

Joseph
106 Greene St.
212.343.7071

Lucky Brand Jeans
38 Greene St.
212.625.0707

Malo
125 Wooster St.

Mare
426 W. Broadway
212.343.1110

Onward
172 Mercer St.
212.274.1255

Phat Farm
129 Prince St.
212.533.7428

Quicksilver
109-111 Spring St.
212.334.4500

Men's Clothes (cont'd)

R by 45 rpm
169 Mercer St.
917.237.0045

Replay
109 Prince St.
212.673.6300

Rugby North America
115 Mercer St.
212.431.3069

Stussy NYC
140 Wooster St.
212.995.8787

Ted Baker NYC
107 Grand St.
212.343.8989

Yohji Yamamoto USA
103 Grand St.
212.966.9066

Yves Saint Laurent
88 Wooster St.
212.274.0522

Pet Supls/Svcs

Alternative Pet Care
33 Howard St.
212.941.5083

Fetch
43 Greenwich Ave. (6th/7th)
212.352.8591

Frenchware
98 Thompson St.
(Prince/Spring)
212.625.3131

Monsac (dog accessories)
339 W. Broadway
www.monsac.com

The Dog Wash
Grooming
177 MacDougal

The Pet Bar
311 E. 60th St.
212.355.2850
www.suttonpets.com

Photography Services

Daniel Stein
500B Grand St.
212.388.1095

Prince & Sullivan 1Hr. Photo
186 Prince St.
212.941.0833

Real Estate

The Halstead Property Company
451 W. Broadway
212.475.4200

Restaurants
(Outdoor Only)

Bistro Le Amis
180 Spring St. (@ Thompson)
212.226.8645

Restaurants (cont'd)

Bubby's Restaurant Bar & Bakery
120 Hudson St.
212.219.0666

Cub Room Cafe
131 Sullivan St. (@ Prince)
212.677.4100

Grey Dog's Coffee
33 Carmine St.
(Bleecker/Bedford)
212.462.0041

Once Upon A Tart
135 Sullivan St.
(Houston/Prince)
212.387.8869

Raoul's
180 Prince St.
(Sullivan/Thompson)
212.966.3518

SoHo Grand Hotel - Grand Bar
310 W. Broadway (@ Grand)
212.965.3000

Restaurants (cont'd)

Space Untitled
133 Greene St.
(Houston/Prince)
212.260.8962

Rugs

Nomad Rugs
470 Broome St.
212.219.3330

Shoes

Camper
125 Prince St.

Cowboy Boot Shoe Repair
4 Prince St.(4 blks E. of B'wy)
212.941.9532

Jenny B.
118 Spring St.
212.343.9575

Shoes (cont'd)

John Fluevog Shoes Ltd.
250 Mulberry St.

Kate Spade
454 Broome St.
212.274.1991

Kerquelen
44 Greene St.
212.431.1771
www.kerquelen.com

Kerquelen
430 W. Broadway
212.226.8313
www.kerquelen.com

Nancy Geist
107 Spring St.
212.925.7192

Prada
750 5th. Ave (56th/57th)
212.664.0010

Sacco
111 Thompson St.
212.925.8010
www.saccoshoes.com

Shoes (cont'd)

Stephanie Kelian
158 Mercer St.
212.925.3077

Women's Accessories

Furla
430 Broadway
212.343.0048

Kate Spade
454 Broome St.

Monsac
339 Broadway
212.925.3237
www.monsac.com

Yvone Christa
107 Mercer St.
212.965.1001
www.yvonechrista.com

Women's Clothes

Afterlife
59 Greene St.
212.625.3167

Agnis B.
79 Greene St.
212.741.2585

Agnis B.
116-118 Prince St.
212.925.4649

Anne Fontaine
93 Greene St.
212.373.3154
www.annefontaine.com

A.P.C.
131 Mercer St.
212.966.9685

Baby Phat
129 Prince St.
212.533.7428

Betsey Johnson
138 Wooster St.
212.995.5048

Women's Clothes (cont'd)

CD Shades
154 Spring St.

Club Monaco
Prince St.
646.533.8930

FCUK
435 W. Broadway

Haneza
93 Grand St.
212.343.9373

Harriet Love
126 Prince St.
212.966.2280

Hugo Boss
132 Greene St.
212.965.1300

Ina
21 Prince St.
212.334.9048

Women's Clothes (cont'd)

Ina
101 Thompson St.
212.941.4757

Joseph
106 Greene St.
212.343.7071

Kirna Zabete
96 Greene St.
212.941.9656

Kors Michael Kors
159 Mercer St.

Lucky Brand Jeans
38 Greene St.
212.625.0707

Mare
426 W. Broadway
212.343.1110

Miu Miu
100 Prince St.
212.334.5156

Women's Clothes (cont'd)

Nicole Miller
134 Prince St.
212.343.1362

Nuovo Melodrom
60 Greene St.
212.219.0013
www.nuovomelodrom.com

Olive Bette's
158 Spring St.
646.613.8772

Onward
172 Mercer St.
212.274.1255

Pleats Please by Issey Miyake
128 Wooster St-212.226.3600
soho@pleats-please.com

Plein Sud
70 Greene St.

Product
71 Mercer St.
212.625.1630

Women's Clothes (cont'd)

Quicksilver
109-111 Spring St.
212.334.4500

R by 45 rpm
169 Mercer St.
917.237.0045

Rampage
127 Prince St.
917.995.9569

Replay
109 Prince St.
212.673.6300

Rugby North America
115 Mercer St.
212.431.3069

Shabby Chic
83 Wooster St.
212.274.9842

Shin Choi
119 Mercer St.
212.625.9202

Women's Clothes (cont'd)

Sisley
469 W. Broadway
212.375.0538

Stussy NYC
140 Wooster St.
212.995.8787

Tardini
142 Wooster St.
212.253.7692

Tehen
91 Greene St.
212.925.4788

Tocca
161 Mercer St.
212.343.3912

Togs SoHo
68 Spring St.
917.237.1882

Ventilo
69 Greene St.
212.625.3660

Women's Clothes (cont'd)

Vivienne Tam
99 Greene St.
212.966.2398

Wolford Boutique
122 Greene St.
212.343.0808

Yohji Yamamoto USA
103 Grand St.
212.966.9066

Misc.

Typogram
71 Spring St.
212.219.9770

"Having A Wonderful Time, Wish You Were Here!"

Now you can take that long deserved holiday and leave your best friend in the right hands. The Wagging Tail makes sure that your dog is lovingly cared for at all time, whether you're gone for two days or two months. We give your pet the little extras that make their stay special, while attended by professionals who are dog people. So have a wonderful time. Enjoy your holiday. You'll get a happy welcome home!

The Wagging Tail features:

Trained, Caring Attendants Always On Site

Ultra-Sanitary, Warm & "Comfy" Conditions

Fabulous 3,000 sq. ft. Indoor Playground Features Rubber, Non-Skid Floors and Cheerful Natural Light to Stimulate Outdoors

State-of-the-Art Air Purification System Insures

Your Dog Comes Home Odor-Free We Work With You! All Special Care Requests Considered

Day Care Includes Choice of Premium Foods For Breakfast & Dinner

We Serve IAMS & EUKANUBA Dog Foods

Registered Veterinarian Always On 24 hr. Call

All of Our Guests Must Have Proof of Vaccinations

Private Bath! (Translation: We'll give your dog a bath - always big fun at home.)

We care for your dog. That's TLC. And what's more, we care about your dog. Doggone Right.

THE WAGGING TAIL :: DOGGIE DAY CARE

TRIBECA, NYC **AT 354 1/2 GREENWICH STREET - 212.285.4900**

Volume Visitation discounts Encouraged - MasterCard/visa Accepted - Open Everyday 7am to 10pm for Drop-Off and Pick-Up

IAMS - Eukanuba

Now Offering Pick-up & delivery

Animal Hospitals

TriBeCa SoHo Animal Hospital
5 Lispenard St. @ Church St.
212.925.6100

Bicycle Shops

Gotham Bikes
112 W. Broadway
212.732.2453
www.gothambikes.com

Cleaners

Laundry Happy Day, Inc.
71 Leonard St.
212.226.8322

Dog Runs

Tribeca Dog Run
Warren St.
(Washington/West Side Hwy)

Eyewear

Worthy Eyes, Ltd.
40 Worth St. (@ Church St.)
212.233.2203

Flowers

1 Hour Flower.com
W. Broadway
800.958.0008
www.1hourflower.com

Anne/Bruno
115 W. Broadway
212.766.5660

Gifts

YHK
11 Jay
St.(Hudson/Greenwich)
212.226.1300

Hardware

Ace of TriBeCa Hardware
160 W. Broadway
212.571.3788

Home Furnishings

Antiqueria TriBeCa
129 Duane St.
212.227.7500
www.antiqueria.com

Inerieurs
149-151 Franklin St.
212.343.0800

John Kelly Furniture Design
77 Franklin St.
212.625.3355
jkfurndsgn@aol.com

Home Furnishings (cont'd)

Totem
71 Franklin St.
212.925.5506

Urban Archaeology
143 Franklin St.
212.431.4646

Whimsy Blue
177 W. Broadway
212.941.8474
www.whimsyblue.com

White
85 White St.
212.964.4694
www.whiteonwhite.com

Hotels

TriBeCa Grand
2 6th Ave.
212.519.6600
www.tribecagrand.com

Kid's

BU and the Duck.com
106 Franklin St.
212.431.9226
www.buandtheduck.com

Shoo Fly
42 Hudson St.
212.406.3270
www.shoofly.com

Men's Clothes

Detour
425-475 W. Broadway
212.625.1820

Mare
426 W. Broadway
212.343.1110

Shoes

Off Canal
365 Broadway
212.226.5873

Parks

Duane Park
Intersection Duane/Hudson

James J. Walker Park
Hudson (Clarkson/Leroy)

Pet Supls/Svcs

Another Barking Zoo
368 1/2 Greenwich St.
(Franklin/N. Moore)
212.233.0226

Beasty Feast
650 Hudson (@ Jane)
212.620.7099

Wagging Tail, The
354 1/2 Greenwich St.
212.285.4900

Photography Services

DPI Photo Lab
87 Franklin St.
212.966.3485

Restaurants
(outdoor only)

Bassets Coffee & Tea
123 W. Broadway (@ Duane)
212.349.1662

Felix
340 W. Broadway (@ Grand)
212.431.0021

i
277 Church St.
212.625.0505

JJA
301 Church St.

Le Pescadou
18 King St. (@6th Ave.)
212.924.3434

Telephone Supls/Svcs

In Touch Wireless
303 Greenwich St.
212.587.0007

Telephone Supls/Svcs (cont'd)

Wireless Warehouse
200 Church St.
212.619.1000

Women's Clothes

Assets London
152 Franklin St.
212.219.8777

Detour
425-475 W. Broadway
212.625.1820

Seam
117 W. Broadway
212.732.9411

Dog Runs

Friends of Union Square Dog Run
SW Corner of Union Square
(13th/Broadway)

Home Furnishings

ABC Carpet
881-888 Broadway
(@19th St.)
212.473.3000

Men's Clothes

Emporio Armani
110 5th Ave.
212.727.3240

Paul Smith
108 5th Ave. (@ 16th)
212.627.9770

Pet Supls/Svcs

Paul Smith
108 5th Ave. (@ 16th)
212.627.9770

Restaurants

The Coffee Shop
29 Union Square (@ 16th)
212.243.7969

Silver Swan
41 E. 20th St
(B'wy/Park Ave. S.)
212.254.3611

Verbena
54 Irving Place (17th/18th)
212.260.5454

Zen Palate
34 Union Square E. (@ 16th)
212.614.9291

Telephone Supls/Svcs

Totally Connected
111 3rd Ave (@ 14th St.)
212.539.9999

Women's Clothes

Emporio Armani
110 5th Ave.
212.727.3240

Paul Smith
108 5th Ave. (@ 16th)
212.627.9770

Variazioni
104 5th Ave.

Zara
101 5th Ave. (@ 17th)
212.741.0555

Animal Hospitals

Animal Medical Center
510 E. 62nd St (York/FDR)
212.838.7053
www.amcny.org

Park East Animal Hospital
52 E. 64th St. (Park/Madison)
212.832.8417

Baked Goods

Three dog Bakery@Z-Spot
969 Madison Ave

Cleaners

Fancy Cleaners & Tailors
1384 2nd Ave.
212.772.9443

Cosmetics

Creed
897 Madison Ave.
212.794.4480

Face Stockholm
687 Madison Ave (@62nd St.)
212.207.8833

L'Occitane
Madison Ave. (@ 80th St.)
212.355.6135

Dog Runs

Carl Schurz Park - Gracie Square
East End Ave. (84th-89th St.)

East River Pavillion
York Ave. (@ 60th St.)
East River
212.755.3288

Eyewear

H.L. Purdy, Inc.
971 Madison Ave
212.794.2509
sales@hlpurdy.com
www.hlpurdy.com

H.L. Purdy, Inc.
1171 Madison Ave
212.249.3997
sales@hlpurdy.com
www.hlpurdy.com

H.L. Purdy, Inc.
1195 Madison Ave
212.737.0371
sales@hlpurdy.com
www.hlpurdy.com

Selima Optique Madison Avenue
899 Madison Ave.
212.988.6690

Gifts

An American Craftsman
1222 2nd Ave.
212.794.3440

Gifts (cont'd)

Caron
675 Madison Ave
212.319.4888

Erwin Pearl
697 Madison Ave
212.753.3155
www.erwinpearl.com

Jacardi
787 Madison Ave. (@ 60th)
212.535.3200

Le Chien @ Trump Plaza
1044 3rd Ave. (@ 61st)
212.861.8100

Not Just For Dogs
244 E. 60th St. (2nd/3rd)

Spectra
903 Madison Ave.
212.744.2255

Home Furnishings

E. Braun & Co.
717 Madison Ave.
212.838.0650

Home Furnishings (cont'd)

Jacardi
787 Madison Ave. (@ 60th)
212.535.3200

Laytner's Linen & Home
237 E. 86th St.
212.996.4439

Hotels

Carlyle Hotel
35 E. 76th St.
212.744.1600

Franklin, The
164 E. 87th St. (@ Lexington)
212.369.1000

Hotel Plaza Athenee
37 E. 64th St. (Park/Madison)
212.734.9100

Hotels (cont'd)

Pierre
2 E. 61st St.
212.838.8000
Small dogs only, please.

Regency Hotel
540 Park Ave.
212.759.4100

Wales Hotel
1295 Madison Ave.
212.876.6000

Jewelry

Alex Gordon Jewelers
1186 3rd Ave. (@ 69th)
212.570.6773

Alex Gordon Jewelers
1022 Madison Ave.
(78th/79th)
212.628.7915

David Yurman
780 Madison Ave.

Jewelry (cont'd)

Elias Lalaounis
733 Madison Ave.
212.439.9400

Lanciani
826 Lexington Ave.
212.832.2092

Lanciani
992 Madison Ave.
212.717.2759

Liliblue
955 Madison Ave.
212.249.5356

Manfredi
737 Madison Ave.
212.734.8710

Michael Ashton
133 Madison Ave. (@74th)
212.517.6655

SoHo Gem
780 Madison Ave.

Vertigo
955 Madison Ave.
212.439.9826

Jewelry (cont'd)

Zig Zag
963 Madison Ave.
212.472.6373

Zig Zag
1336A 3rd Ave.
212.794.3178

Kid's

Bon Point
811 Madison Ave.
212.879.0900

Bon Point
1269 Madison Ave.
212.722.7720

Calypso
935 Madison Ave.
212.535.4100

Greenstones & CIE
442 Columbus Ave.
212.580.4322

Kid's (cont'd)

Loro Piana
821 Madison Ave.

Moschino
803 Madison Ave.
212.639.9600

Prince & Princess
33 E. 68th St.
212.879.8989

Men's Accessories

Bottega Veneta
655 Madison Ave
212.371.5511

Calypso
935 Madison Ave.
212.535.4100

Emporio Armani
601 Madison Ave.
212.317.0800

Ilias Lalaounis
733 Madison Ave.
212.439.9400

Men's Accessories (cont'd)

Krizia
769 Madison Ave
212.879.1211

L'Occitane
Madison Ave. (@ 80th St.)
212.355.6135

Lana Marks
645 Madison Ave
212.355.6135

Prada
841 Madison Ave (@70th)
212.327.4200

Roberto Cavalli
711 Madison Ave.

Robert Cler Gerie
681 Madison Ave.
212.207.8600

Scully & Scully Park Ave.
504 Park Ave. (59th/60th)
212.327.4200

Men's Accessories (cont'd)

Sergio Rossi
835 Madison Ave.
212.396.4814

Stephane Kelian
717 Madison Ave.
212.980.1919

Valentino
747 Madison Ave.
212.772.6969

Men's Clothes

Barney's New York
Madison Ave. at 61st St.
212.826.8900

Bergdorf Goodman
754 5th Ave. (@58th St.)
212.753.7300

Bloomingdale's
1000 3rd Ave. (59th/60th)
212.705.2000

Men's Clothes (cont'd)

Bottega Veneta
655 Madison Ave
212.371.5511

Burberry London
9 E. 57th St. (Madison/5th)
212.371.5010

Calypso
935 Madison Ave.
212.535.4100

Cerruti
789 Madison Ave.
212.327.2222

Club Monaco
65th St. (@ 3rd Ave.)
646.533.8930

DKNY
655 Madison Ave. (@60th St.)
212.223.3569

Emporio Armani
601 Madison Ave.
212.317.0800

Men's Clothes (cont'd)

Gia Franco Ferre
845 Madison Ave.
212.717.5430

Gianni Versace
815 Madison Ave.
212.744.6868

Gucci
685 5th Ave. (@54th)
212.826.2600

Issey Miyake
992 Madison Ave.
212.439.7822
madison@isseymiyake.com

Krizia
769 Madison Ave
212.879.1211

Michael Kors
974 Madison Ave.
212.452.4685

Moschino
803 Madison Ave.
212.639.9600

Men's Clothes (cont'd)

Robert Marc
782 Madison Ave.
212.737.6000

Robert Marc
1046 Madison Ave.
212.988.9600

Robert Marc
1300 Madison Ave.
212.722.1600

Roberto Cavalli
711 Madison Ave.

Super Runners Shop
1246 3rd Ave.
212.249.2133

Super Runners Shop
1337 Lexington Ave.
212.369.6010

Tse
827 Madison Ave.
212.472.7790

Valentino
747 Madison Ave.
212.772.6969

Men's Clothes (cont'd)

Versace
815 Madison Ave.
212.744.6868

Opticians

Morganthal Fredrics
699 Madison Ave.
212.838.3090

Parks

Carl Schurz Park
Gracie Square (84th/89th)

Conservatory Garden
105th St. (@ 5th Ave.)
:00 am to dusk daily

Pet Supls/Svcs

Karen's "For People & Pets"
1195 Lexington (81st/82nd)
212.472.9440

Le Chien @ Trump Plaza
1044 3rd Ave. (@ 61st)
212.861.8100

Not Just For Dogs
244 E. 60th St. (2nd/3rd)

Run Spot Run, Inc. Dog Spa
415 E. 91st St. (1st/York)
212.966.6666

Sutton dog Parlour
311 E. 60th St.
212.355.2850
www.suttonpets.com

Zitomer Z Spot
132 Thompson St.
(Houston/Prince)
212.253.9250

Real Estate

Douglas Elliman
980 Madison Ave.
212.650.4800
www.douglaselliman.com

Fenwick-Keats Downtown, LLC
1185 Lexington Ave. (@80th)

Restaurants (outside only)

Atlantic Grill
1431 3rd Ave.
212.988.9200

Baraonda
1439 2nd Ave. (@ 74th)
212.288.8555

Barking Dog Luncheonette
1678 3rd Ave. (@ 94th)
212.831.1800

Restaurants (cont'd)

Bistro du Nord
1312 Madison Ave. (@ 93rd)
212.289.0997

Cafe Nosidam
768 Madison Ave. (@ 66th)
212.717.5633

Cinema
1325 2nd Ave.
212.772.6400
www.cinemarestaurants.com

Ciao Bella Cafe
27 E. 92nd St. (5th/Madison)
212.831.5555

Coconut Grill
1481 2nd Ave.
212.772.6262

Ferrier
29 E. 65th St. (off Madison)
212.772.9000

Ice Cream Cafe
Central Park (72nd/5th Ave.)

Restaurants (cont'd)

Leaping Frog Cafe
830 5th Ave. (@ 64th St.)
212.717.8918

Le Petit Hulot
973 Lexington
Ave.(70th/71st)
212.794.9800

Merchant's
1125 1st Ave.

Merchant's
1608 1st Ave.

Park View at the Boathouse
Central Pk (72nd/E.Park Dr.N)
212.517.2233

Pascalou
1308 Madison Ave(92nd/93rd)
212.534.7522

Vespa Cibobuono
1625 2nd Ave (84th/85th)
212.472.2050

Restaurants (cont'd)

Zocalo
174 E. 82nd St. (3rd/Lex)
212.717.7772

Shoes

Bati
105L 3rd Ave. (62nd/63rd)

Bottega Veneta
655 Madison Ave
212.371.5511

Maraolo
1321 3rd Ave
212.535.6225

Prada
841 Madison Ave (@70th)
212.327.4200

Rapax
1100 Madison Ave
212.734.5171

Shoes (cont'd)

Roberto Cavalli
711 Madison Ave.

Robert Cler Gerie
681 Madison Ave.
212.207.8600

Sergio Rossi
835 Madison Ave.
212.396.4814

Stephane Kelian
717 Madison Ave.
212.980.1919

Stuart Weitzman
625 Madison Ave
212.750.2555

Super Runners Shop
1246 3rd Ave.
212.249.2133

Super Runners Shop
1337 Lexington Ave.
212.369.6010

Via Spiga
765 Madison Ave.
212.988.4877

Telephone Supls/Svcs

Totally Connected
352 E. 86th St.
212.794.5200

Women's Accessories

Bebe
1044 Madison Ave.
212.517.2323

Bebe
1127 3rd Ave.
212.935.2444

Bottega Veneta
655 Madison Ave
212.371.5511

Calypso
935 Madison Ave.
212.535.4100

Celine
667 Madison Ave.
212.486.9700

Women's Accessories (cont'd)

Emporio Armani
601 Madison Ave.
212.317.0800

Furla
727 Madison Ave.
212.755.8986

Genny
831 Madison Ave.
212.249.9660

Ilias Lalaounis
733 Madison Ave.
212.439.9400

Krizia
769 Madison Ave
212.879.1211

Lana Marks
645 Madison Ave
212.355.6135

Loro Piana
821 Madison Ave.

Women's Accessories (cont'd)

Prada
841 Madison Ave (@70th)
212.327.4200

Roberto Cavalli
711 Madison Ave.

Robert Cler Gerie
681 Madison Ave.
212.207.8600

Scully & Scully Park Ave.
504 Park Ave. (59th/60th)
212.327.4200

Sergio Rossi
835 Madison Ave.
212.396.4814

Sonia Rykiel
849 Madison Ave.
212.396.3060

Stephane Kelian
717 Madison Ave.
212.980.1919

Women's Accessories (cont'd)

Via Spiga
765 Madison Ave.
212.988.4877

Wolford
619 Madison Ave. (@ 77th)
212.688.4850

Worldly Things
837 Madison Ave.
212.988.7810

Women's Clothes

Agnis B.
1063 Madison Ave.
212.570.9333

BCBG Max Mara
813 Madison Ave.
212.879.6100

Women's Clothes (cont'd)

Barney's New York
Madison Ave. at 61st St.
212.826.8900

Bebe
1044 Madison Ave.
212.517.2323

Bebe
1127 3rd Ave.
212.935.2444

Bergdorf Goodman
754 5th Ave. (@58th St.)
212.753.7300

Betsey Johnson
1060 Madison Ave.
212.734.1257

Bloomingdale's
1000 3rd Ave. (59th/60th)
212.705.2000

Bottega Veneta
655 Madison Ave
212.371.5511

Women's Clothes (cont'd)

Burberry London
9 E. 57th St. (Madison/5th)
212.371.5010

Calypso
935 Madison Ave.
212.535.4100

Celine
667 Madison Ave.
212.486.9700

Cerruti
789 Madison Ave.
212.327.2222

Club Monaco
65th St. (@ 3rd Ave.)
646.533.8930

DKNY
655 Madison Ave. (@60th St.)
212.223.3569

Emporio Armani
601 Madison Ave.
212.317.0800

Women's Clothes (cont'd)

Ensoie
988 Madison Ave.
212.717.7958

Episode
625 Madison Ave.
212.755.6061

Eres
621 Madison Ave.
212.223.3550

Fogal
680 Madison Ave. (@ 61st)
212.355.3254
info@fogal.com

Genny
831 Madison Ave.
212.249.9660

Gia Franco Ferre
845 Madison Ave.
212.717.5430

Gianni Versace
815 Madison Ave.
212.744.6868

Women's Clothes (cont'd)

Gucci
685 5th Ave. (@54th)
212.826.2600

Issey Miyake
992 Madison Ave.
212.439.7822
madison@isseymiyake.com

Joseph
796 Madison Ave
212.327.1773

Joseph
804 Madison Ave
212.570.0077

Krizia
769 Madison Ave
212.879.1211

Loro Piana
821 Madison Ave.

Michael Kors
974 Madison Ave.
212.452.4685

Women's Clothes (cont'd)

Moga
715 Madison Ave.
212.751.7506

Moschino
803 Madison Ave.
212.639.9600

Olive Bette's
1070 Madison Ave.
212.717.9566

Robert Marc
782 Madison Ave.
212.737.6000

Robert Marc
1046 Madison Ave.
212.988.9600

Robert Marc
1300 Madison Ave.
212.722.1600

Roberto Cavalli
711 Madison Ave.

Women's Clothes (cont'd)

Sonia Rykiel
849 Madison Ave.
212.396.3060

Super Runners Shop
1246 3rd Ave.
212.249.2133

Super Runners Shop
1337 Lexington Ave.
212.369.6010

Tse
827 Madison Ave.
212.472.7790

Valentino
747 Madison Ave.
212.772.6969

Versace
815 Madison Ave.
212.744.6868

Vertigo
755 Madison Ave.
212.439.9826

Women's Clothes (cont'd)

Wolford
619 Madison Ave. (@ 77th)
212.688.4850

Worldly Things
837 Madison Ave.
212.988.7810

Yves Saint Laurent
855 Madison Ave.
212.988.3821

Zara
750 Lexington Ave. (@ 59th)
212.754.1120

Misc.

Sharper Image
900 Madison Ave.

Animal Hospitals

Westside Veterinary Center
220 W. 83rd St. (Amst/Bwy)
212.580.1800

Bicycle Shops

Bicycle Renaissance
430 Columbus Ave. (@ 81st)
212.724.2350
212.580.0751
212.362.3388

Eddie's Bicycle Shop
490 Amsterdam Ave.
212.580.2011

Toga!
110 West End Ave.
212.799.9625
www.togabikes.com

Dog Runs

Canine Court Van Courtland Park
W. 252nd St. (@ Broadway)

Central Park
Central Park W. - 5th Ave.
59th - 110th St.

Riverside Park
Riverside Drive
(@ 77th, 87th, 105th, 121st)

Theodore Roosevelt Park - Teddy's Dog Run
81st St. (@ Columbus Ave.)

Eyewear

Euro Optika
333 W. 57th St. (8th/9th)
212.262.5757

Euro Optika
288 Columbus Ave(73rd/74th)
212.501.7070

Eyewear (cont'd)

Eye Q Optometrist
381 Amsterdam Ave.
212.724.8855
www.eyehoo.com

Ideal Eyes, Inc.
2301 Broadway
212.787.8477

Sun Goddess
473 Amsterdam Ave.
(82nd/83rd)
917.441.4141

The Eye Man, LTD
2264 Broadway (81st/82nd)
212.873.4114

Frames

Gallery II Collections, Inc.
2244 Broadway
212.877.9780

Frames (cont'd)

LaBelle Epoque
280 Columbus Ave. (@ 73rd)
212.362.1770
posters@la-belle-epoque.com
www.la-belle-epoque.com

Gifts

Bath Island
469 Amsterdam Ave.
212.787.9415
bathisland@netscape.net
www.bathisland.com

Body Shop, The
76th St. (@ Broadway)

Cardeology
314 Columbus Ave.
(74th/75th)
212.579.9310

Cardeology
452 Amsterdam Ave.
(81st/82nd)
212.873.2491

Country Corner
196 Columbus Ave.

Gifts (cont'd)

Laura Ashley, Inc.
398 Columbus Ave.
212.496.5110

Tibet Bazaar
473 Amsterdam Ave.
(82nd/83rd)
212.595.8487

Home Furnishings

Door Store
601 Amsterdam Ave.
212.501.8696

Laura Ashley, Inc.
398 Columbus Ave.
212.496.5110

Laytner's
2270 Broadway (@ 81st)
212.724.0180
www.laytners.com

Metropolitan Design Center
2200 Broadway (@ 78th)
212.712.2258
212.712.2097

Jewelry

Alex Gordon Jewelers
2328 Broadway (84th/85th)
212.724.8710

Alex Gordon Jewelers
2230 Columbus Ave.
(70th/71st)
212.721.4368

Daphne
467 Amsterdam Ave.
212.877.5073
www.daphne1.com

Roslyn
276 Columbus Ave.
212.496.5050

Tibet Bazaar
473 Amsterdam Ave.
(82nd/83rd)
212.595.8487

Kid's

Cradle & All
110 W. 86th St.
212.580.3801
www.cradleandallnyc.com

Kid's (cont'd)

Granny Made
381 Amsterdam Ave.
(78th/79th)
212.496.1222
www.granny-made.com

Greenstones & CIE
442 Columbus Ave.
212.580.4322

ShooFly
465 Amsterdam Ave.
212.580.4390

Tip Top Kids
149 W. 72nd St.
212.874.1004

Men's Accessories

Bath Island
469 Amsterdam Ave.
212.787.9415
bathisland@netscape.net
www.bathisland.com

Men's Accessories (cont'd)

Body Shop, The
76th St. (@ Broadway)

Roslyn
276 Columbus Ave.
212.496.5050

Tano
2286 Broadway (82nd/83rd)
212.362.5070

Tibet Bazaar
473 Amsterdam Ave.
(82nd/83rd)
212.595.8487

Men's Clothes

Bath Island
469 Amsterdam Ave.
212.787.9415
bathisland@netscape.net
www.bathisland.com

Men's Clothes (cont'd)

Club Monaco
2376 Broadway
212.579.2587

Frank Stella Clothiers
440 Columbus Ave. (@ 81st)
646.877.5566

Granny Made
381 Amsterdam Ave.
(78th/79th)
212.496.1222
www.granny-made.com

Super Runners Shop
360 Amsterdam Ave.
212.787.7665

Tibet Bazaar
473 Amsterdam Ave.
(82nd/83rd)
212.595.8487

Opticians

Eye Q Optometrist
381 Amsterdam Ave.
212.724.8855
www.eyehoo.com

Parks

Dante Park
Lincoln Center
(65th/Columbus)

Edgar Allan Poe St.
84th St.
(Riverside - Broadway)

Park & Garden, Garden
55-57 W. 87th St.
(Central Park W. - Columbus)

Riverside Park
Riverside Dr.
(W. 72nd - 158th)

West End Towers Park
75 West End Ave. (63rd/64th)

Pet Supls/Svcs

Amsterdog Groomers
586 Amsterdam (88th/89th)
212.496.6117

Animal General
558 Columbus Ave.
212.501.9600

Pet Supls/Svcs (cont'd)

Follow My Lead Dog Training
117 W. 74th St.
212.873.5511

Pet Bowl
440 Amsterdam (@ 81st)
212.595.4200

Pet Market, The
210 W. 72nd St.
(Broadway/West End Ave.)
212.799.4200

Pet Shop
564 Columbus Ave.
212.580.2400

Photography Services

Spectra Photo/Digital
451 Amsterdam
212.362.0094
spectranyc@earthlink.net
www.spectra-nyc.com

Real Estate

The Corcoran Group
2253 Broadway
212.875.2979
www.corcoran.com

Restaurants

(outdoor only)

Artie's New York
2290 Broadway (82nd/83rd)
212.579.5959

Avenue
520 Columbus Ave.
212.579.3194

Bella Luna
584 Columbus Ave.
(@ 89th St.)
212.877.2267

Boulevard
2398 Broadway (@ 88th St.)
212.874.7400

Cafe Mozart
154 W. 70th St.
(@ Broadway)
212.595.9797

Restaurants (cont'd)

Columbus Cafe
556 Columbus Ave.
(86th/87th)
212.721.9040

Firehouse
522 Columbus Ave.
(85th/86th)
212.787.3473

Fountain Cafe
Lincoln Center
(65th/Columbus)
212.874.7000

Isabella's
359 Columbus Ave.
212.724.2100

Josephina
1900 Broadway (63rd/64th)
212.799.1000

Merchant's
521 Columbus Ave. (@ 85th)
212.721.3689

Restaurants (cont'd)

Metisse
239 W. 105th St.
(Amsterdam/Broadway)
212.666.8825

Mineral Springs Cafe
Central Park (70th@West Dr.)

North West
392 Columbus Ave.
212.799.4530

Ocean Grill
384 Columbus Ave.
212.579.2300

Opera Espresso Cafe
1928 Broadway (64th/65th)
212.799.3050

Pappardella
316 Columbus Ave.
212.595.7996

Tavern On The Green
Central Park West (66th/67th)
212.873.3200

Shoes

Bati
2323 Broadway (84th/85th)
212.724.7214

Montmartre
2212 Broadway
212.875.8430

Montmartre
247 Columbus Ave.
212.721.7760

Profiles
294 Columbus Ave. (@ 74th)
212.799.1994
siriam@webtv.net

Sacco
2355 Broadway (@ 86th)
212.874.8362
www.saccoshoes.com

Sacco
324 Columbus Ave.
212.799.5229
www.saccoshoes.com

Steve Madden
2315 Broadway
212.799.4221
www.stevemadden.com

Shoes (cont'd)

Super Runners Shop
360 Amsterdam Ave.
212.787.7665

Tani
131 W. 72nd St.
212.595.1338
www.tanishoes.com

Tano
2286 Broadway (82nd/83rd)
212.362.5070

Telephone Supls/Svcs

Wireless Solutions
324 Columbus Ave.
(75th/76th)
212.496.9515

Women's Accessories

Bath Island
469 Amsterdam Ave.
212.787.9415
bathisland@netscape.net
www.bathisland.com

Women's Accessories (cont'd)

Body Shop, The
76th St. (@ Broadway)

Laura Ashley, Inc.
398 Columbus Ave.
212.496.5110

Liana
324 Columbus Ave.
(75th/76th)
212.873.8746

Montmartre
2212 Broadway
212.875.8430

Montmartre
247 Columbus Ave.
212.721.7760

Off Broadway Boutique
139 W. 72nd St.
212.724.6713

Really Great Things
284A Columbus Ave.
212.787.5354

Women's Accessories (cont'd)

Roslyn
276 Columbus Ave.
212.496.5050

Tibet Bazaar
473 Amsterdam Ave.
(82nd/83rd)
212.595.8487

Zan Boutique
2394 Broadway
212.877.4853

Women's Clothes

Assets London
464 Columbus Ave.
212.874.8253

Bath Island
469 Amsterdam Ave.
212.787.9415
bathisland@netscape.net
www.bathisland.com

Women's Clothes (cont'd)

Betsey Johnson
24 Columbus Ave.

Capry Uomo
105 W. 72nd St.
212.724.7500

CD Shades
300 Columbus Ave.

Club Monaco
2376 Broadway
212.579.2587

Darryl's
490-492 Amsterdam Ave.
(83rd/84th)
212.874.6677
212.721.2709

FCUK
1270 6th Ave.

FCUK
700 Broadway

FCUK
304 Columbus Ave.

Women's Clothes (cont'd)

Frank Stella Clothiers
440 Columbus Ave. (@ 81st)
646.877.5566

Granny Made
381 Amsterdam Ave.
(78th/79th)
212.496.1222
www.granny-made.com

Laina Jane Lingerie
416 Amsterdam Ave.
212.727.7032

Laura Ashley, Inc.
398 Columbus Ave.
212.496.5110

Liana
324 Columbus Ave.
(75th/76th)
212.873.8746

Montmartre
2212 Broadway
212.875.8430

Women's Clothes (cont'd)

Montmartre
247 Columbus Ave.
212.721.7760

Off Broadway Boutique
139 W. 72nd St.
212.724.6713

Olive Bette's
252 Columbus Ave (@ 72nd)
212.579.2178

Really Great Things
284A Columbus Ave.
212.787.5354

Sisley
2308 Broadway
212.769.0121

Super Runners Shop
360 Amsterdam Ave.
212.787.7665

Tibet Bazaar
473 Amsterdam Ave.
(82nd/83rd)
212.595.8487

Women's Clothes (cont'd)

Zan Boutique
2394 Broadway
212.877.4853

Zara
34th St - 39th St.
(@ 5th Ave.)
212.868.6551

Cosmetics

Sephora
212.629.9135

Dog Runs

DeWitt Clinton Park
Main run -52nd St. (@11th Ave.)
11th Ave. (@54th)

Hell's Kitchen Dog Run
10th Ave. (39th/40th)
212.736.4536

Eyewear

Morganthal Fredrics
754 5th Ave.
Bergdorf Goodman (Plaza Lvl)
212.872.2526

Gifts

An American Craftsman
60 W. 50th St.
212.586.3091

Gifts (cont'd)

An American Craftsman
790 7th Ave.
212.399.2555

Hotels

Renaissance New York Hotel
714 7th Ave.
212.765.7676
Small & Medium dogs only

Mainsfield
12 W. 44th St.
212.944.6050

Men's Accessories

Hermes
11 E. 57th St. (6th/7th)
212.751.3181

Men's Accessories (cont'd)

Prada
750 5th Ave. (56th/57th)
212.664.0010

Men's Clothes

Frank Stella Clothiers
921 7th Ave. (@ 58th St.)
646.957.1600

Hermes
11 E. 57th St. (6th/7th)
212.751.3181

Parks

Bryant Park
Avenue of the Americas
(40th - 42nd)

Parks (cont'd)

Clinton Community Garden
436 W. 48th St. (9th/10th)

Restaurants
(Outdoor Only)

Brasserie Centrale
1700 Broadway (@ 53rd)
212.757.2233

Bryant Park Cafe
25 W. 40th St.
(@ Ave. of the Americas)
212.840.6500

Puttanesca
859 9th Ave. (@56th)
212.581.4177

Rue 57
60 W. 57th St.
(@ Ave. of the Americas)
212.307.5656

Seppi's
123 W. 56th St. (6th/7th)
212.708.7444

Telephone Supls/Svcs

Mobile City
299 Broadway
212.385.5353

Mobile City
526 7th Ave.

Mobile City
1230 6th Ave.

Women's Accessories

Hermes
11 E. 57th St. (6th/7th)
212.751.3181

Prada
750 5th Ave. (56th/57th)
212.664.0010

Zan Boutique
1666 Broadway (51st/52nd)
212.582.5580

Women's Clothes

Frank Stella Clothiers
921 7th Ave. (@ 58th St.)
646.957.1600

Hermes
11 E. 57th St. (6th/7th)
212.751.3181

Zan Boutique
1666 Broadway (51st/52nd)
212.582.5580

Animal Hospitals

West Village Veterinary Hospital
705-A Washington St.
212.633.7400

West Village Veterinary Hospital
11 Perry St.
212.633.7400

Aromatherapy

Enfluerage
321 Bleecker St.
212.691.1610

Baked Goods

Colette's Cakes
681 Washington St.
(10th/Charles)
212.366.6530

Dog Runs

West Village D.O.G.
Gansevoort (West Side Hwy - Washington St.)
212.807.0093
www.wvdog.org

Washington Square Park - George's Run
W. 4th St.
(Thompson - McDougal)

Eyewear

Desiron
139 W. 22nd St.
212.414.4070
www.desiron.com

My Optics
96 7th Ave
212.633.6054

My Optics
82 Christopher St.
212.741.9550

Gifts

Charley and Kelley
353 Bleecker St.
212.414.0638

Details
347 Bleecker St. (@ 10th St.)
212.414.0039

DVVS
263A W. 19th St.
212.366.4888
www.dvvs.com

Enchanted Candle
22 Greenwich Ave.
212.924.1101
webmaster@enchantedcandle.com
www.enchantedcandle.com

Hudson Street Papers
357 Bleecker St.

Le Gamin
114 W. Houston St.
646.654.6685

London Boutique
35 Christopher St.
212.647.9106

Gifts (cont'd)

Rainbows & Triangles
192 8th Ave.
212.627.2166

Roger & Dave
123 7th Ave.
212.989.1184

Roger & Dave
224 8th Ave.
212.645.4563

The Alternative
85 Christopher St.
212.645.8966

Jewelry

Eastern Arts
365 Bleecker St.
212.929.7460

Charley and Kelley
353 Bleecker St.
212.414.0638

DVVS
263A W. 19th St.
212.366.4888
www.dvvs.com

Jewelry (cont'd)

Gallery Eclectic
43 Greenwich Ave.
212.924.4314

Graphic Village Wear
87 Christopher St.
212.929.0688

Yamak, Inc.
321 1/2 Bleecker St.
(Christopher/Grove)
212.807.9100

Liquor Stores

Spirits of Carmine
52 Carmine St.
212.206.0091

Men's Accessories

Graphic Village Wear
87 Christopher St.
212.929.0688

Men's Clothes

Fashion Storm, Inc.
306 Bleecker St.
212.414.4080

Gerry's Menswear
110 8th Ave.
212.243.9141

Gerry's Menswear
353 Bleecker St.
212.243.9233

Graphic Village Wear
87 Christopher St.
212.929.0688

Loft
89 Christopher St.
212.691.2334

L'Uomo
383 Bleecker St.
212.206.1844

Marc Jacobs
403 Bleecker St.
212.924.0026

Starting Line, The
180 8th Ave.
212.691.4729

Men's Clothes (cont'd)

World
22 8th Ave.
212.206.8880

World
5 Christopher St.
212.675.1364

Music

Bleecker St. Records
239 Bleecker St.
212.255.7899

Kim's Video & Music
144 Bleecker St.
212.387.8250
info@kimsvideo.com

Kim's Video & Music
350 Bleecker St.
212.675.8996
info@kimsvideo.com

London Boutique
5 Christopher St.
212.647.9106

Parks

Christopher Park
Sheridan Sq. (Christopher -
Grove @ 7th Ave.)

Washington Square Park
W. 4th St.
(Thompson - McDougal)

Pet Supls/Svcs

American Dog Trainers Network
161 W. 4th St. (5th/6th)

Beasty Feast
630 Hudson St. (@ Jane St.)
212.620.7099

Beasty Feast
237 Bleecker St. (@ 6th Ave.)
212.243.3261

Beasty Feast
680 Washington St.
(@ Charles St.)
212.620.4055

Pet Supls/Svcs (cont'd)

Beverly Hills Launder Mutt
45 Grove St.
212.691.7700

Bonnie's K-9 Swim Center
136 9th Ave. (18th/19th)
212.414.2500

Fetch
43 Greenwich Ave.
212.352.8591

Four Paws Club, The
387 Bleecker St.
212.367.8265

Groom-O-Rama, Inc.
496 6th Ave (12th/13th)
212.627.2899

Heart of Chelsea Animal Hospital
257 W. 18th St.
212.924.6116

Pet Supls/Svcs (cont'd)

New York Bed & Biscuit
5th Ave (@ Washington Sq.)
212.475.6064

Poodle Cut, The
14 Bedford St.
212.929.0137

Urban Bird
19 Greenwich St.
212.352.3332
www.urbanbird.com

Urban Pets
18 Christopher St.
212.828.4254

Photography Services

Taranto Labs
245 W. 19th St.
212.691.6070
ken@tarantolab.com

Real Estate

Roomates, NYC
168 W. 22nd St.
212.627.1871
www.roomates-nyc.com

Restaurants
(outdoor only)

Antonio
140 W. 13th St. (6th/7th)
212.645.4606

Arte
21 E. 9th St. (5th/University)
212.473.0077

Arte Pasta
81 Greenwich Ave. (Bank/7th)
212.229.0234

Bandito
33 Greenwich Ave.
212.807.0120

Bar Six
502 6th Ave. (12th/13th)
212.691.1363

Restaurants (cont'd)

Cafe San Marco
211 Waverly Pl. (7th/Charles)
212.367.7535

Chez Ma Tante
189 W. 10th St.
(Bleecker/7th)
212.620.0223

Cowgirl Hall of Fame
519 Hudson St. (@ 10th St.)
212.633.1133

Cuisine de Saigon
154 W. 13th St. (6th/7th)
212.255.6003

Da Silvano
260 6th Ave.
(Bleecker/Houston)
212.982.2343

Dew Drop Inn
57 Greenwich Ave.
212.924.8055

French Roast
78 W. 11th St. (@ 6th Ave.)
212.533.2233

Restaurants (cont'd)

Greenwich Street Cafe
75 Greenwich Ave.
(@ 7th Ave.)
212.255.5450

LeGans
842 Greenwich St.
212.675.5224

Les Deux Gamins
170 Waverly Pl. (@ Grove St.)
212.807.7357

Markt
401 W. 14th St. (@ 9th Ave.)
212.727.3314

Magnolio Bakery
401 Bleecker St. (@ 11th St.)
212.462.2572

Pastis
9 Ninth Ave.
(@ Little W. 12th St.)
212.929.4844

Philip Marie
569 Hudson St. (@ W. 11th)
212.242.6200

Restaurants (cont'd)

Salam Cafe & Restaurant
104 W. 13th St. (6th/7th)
212.741.0277

Sapore
55 Greenwich St.
212.229.0551

Sud
210 W. 10th St.
(Bleecker/W. 4th)
212.255.3805

Tartine
253 W. 11th St. (@ W. 4th)
212.229.2611

Salons

Mario Nico
266 W. 22nd St.
212.727.8464

Shoes

London Boutique
85 Christopher St.
212.647.9106

Telephone Supls/Svcs

Wireless
Greenwich Ave.
212.647.0212

Video

Kim's Video & Music
144 Bleecker St.
212.260.1010
info@kimsvideo.com

Kim's Video & Music
50 Bleecker St.
212.675.8996
info@kimsvideo.com

Video (cont'd)

London Boutique
85 Christopher St.
212.647.9106

World of Video
510 Greenwich Ave.
212.627.1095

Women's Accessories

Yamak, Inc.
321 1/2 Bleecker St.
(Christopher/Grove)
212.807.9100

Women's Clothes

Arleen Bowman
353 Bleecker St.
212.645.8740

Women's Clothes (cont'd)

Laina Jane Lingerie
35 Christopher St.
212.727.7032

London Boutique
85 Christopher St.
212.647.9106

Sleek on Bleecker
361 Bleecker St.
212.243.0284
sleek@att.net

Yamak, Inc.
321 1/2 Bleecker St.
(Christopher/Grove)
212.807.9100

Misc.

Condomania
351 Bleecker St.
212.691.9442

Misc. (cont'd)

Enfluerage
321 Bleecker St.
212.691.1610

Flightool
96 Greenwich Ave.
212.691.0001

Home Furnishings

Door Store
www.doorstorefurniture.com

Men's Accessories

Coach
212.754.0041

Parks

Hudson River
Battery Park - 141st St.

Pet Supls/Svcs

Michael Catron
646.33.7769

Petland Discounts
Over 100 locations

Real Estate

Douglas Elliman
212.650.4800

Halstead Property Group
51 W. Broadway
212.475.4200

Rezanamazi Real Estate
www.rezanamazirealestate.com

Transportation

Hampton Jitney
800.936.0440
All dogs must be in carrier.
Small dogs only.

Hampton Limo
800.936.0440
Press #5

Long Island Railroad
Penn Station
34th St./7th Ave.
718.217.5477

Transportation (cont'd)

New York Water Taxi
212.681.8111

Women's Accessories

Coach
212.754.0041

Women's Clothes

Ann Taylor
All Locations

Talbot's
All Locations

Misc.

Mail Boxes, Etc.
All Locations

*Category Listings
By Neighborhood*

SoHo

TriBeCa SoHo Animal Hospital
5 Lispenard
St(Church/W.Bwy)
212.925.6100

TriBeCa

TriBeCa SoHo Animal Hospital
5 Lispenard St. @ Church St.
212.925.6100

Upper East Side

Animal Medical Center
510 E. 62nd St (York/FDR)
212.838.7053
www.amcny.org

Park East Animal Hospital
52 E. 64th St. (Park/Madison)
212.832.8417

Upper West Side

Westside Veterinary Center
220 W. 83rd St. (Amst/Bwy)
212.580.1800

West Village

West Village Veterinary Hospital
705-A Washington St.
212.633.7400

West Village Veterinary Hospital
11 Perry St.
212.633.7400

SoHo

AIX
462 Broome St.
212.941.7919

Alice's Antiques
72 Greene St.

Paterae
458 Broome St.
212.941.0880

SoHo

Illuminations
54 Spring St.

212.226.8713

West Village

Enfluerage
321 Bleecker St.
212.691.1610

Baked Goods

Upper East Side

Three dog Bakery@Z-Spot
169 Madison Ave

West Village

Colette's Cakes
81 Washington St.
(10th/Charles)
212.366.6530

TriBeCa

Gotham Bikes
112 W. Broadway
212.732.2453
www.gothambikes.com

Upper West Side

Bicycle Renaissance
430 Columbus Ave. (@ 81st)
212.724.2350
212.580.0751
212.362.3388

Eddie's Bicycle Shop
490 Amsterdam Ave.
212.580.2011

Toga!
110 West End Ave.
212.799.9625
www.togabikes.com

SoHo

OK Cigars
383A W. Broadway
212.965.9065

East 23rd - 59th St.

Fancy Cleaners & Tailors
384 3rd Ave.
212.481.1112

Fancy Cleaners & Tailors
1087 2nd Ave.
212.223.7455

Fancy Cleaners & Tailors
254 3rd Ave.
212.982.2007

Fancy Cleaners & Tailors
860-870 UN Plaza Vale
212.759.2006

East Village

Fancy Cleaners & Tailors
176 2nd Ave.
212.677.7757

East Village (cont'd)

Fancy Cleaners & Tailors
40 E. 8th St.
212.358.1133

Kim's Cleaners
99 Ave. A
212.260.0697

Young's Cleaners
17th St. (@ 3rd Ave.)
212.473.6154

TriBeCa

Laundry Happy Day, Inc.
71 Leonard St.
212.226.8322

Upper East Side

Fancy Cleaners & Tailors
1384 2nd Ave.
212.772.9443

East 23rd - 59th St.

Tower Copy
27 3rd Ave.
212.679.3509
www.inch.com/~tce

East 23rd - 59th St.

Aveda
509 Madison Ave
212.832.2416

Qiora
535 Madison Ave
212.527.9933

Sephora
212.245.1633

Flatiron

Aveda
140 5th Ave.
212.645.4797

Sephora
212.674.3570

SoHo

Aveda
233 Spring St.
212.807.1490

Aveda
456 W. Broadway
212.473.0280

Creed
9 Bond St.

Face Stockholm
110 Prince St.
212.966.9110

MAC
212.334.4641

Max Studio
415 W. Broadway
212.941.1141
www.maxstudio.com

Sephora
212.625.1309

SoHo (cont'd)

Shideido Cosmetics, Ltd.
98 Prince St.
212.925.7880

Upper East Side

Creed
897 Madison Ave.
212.794.4480

Face Stockholm
687 Madison Ave (@62nd St.)
212.207.8833

L'Occitane
Madison Ave. (@ 80th St.)
212.355.6135

West 23rd - 59th St.

Sephora
212.629.9135

Chelsea

Chelsea Waterside Park
22nd St.
(11th Ave./West Side Hwy)

Hudson Esplanade Walk
Between Chelsea Piers &
Battery Park.

East 23rd – 59th St.

Peter Detmold Park
Beekman Pl
(49th - 51st @ FDR Drive)

Robert Moses Park
42nd St. (1st Ave/FDR Drive)

Madison Square Park
25th St. (@ Madison Ave.)

East Village

Fish Bridge Park
Dover St.
(Pearl/Water off Bklyn Bridge)

Tompkins Square Park
1st Ave. & Ave. B (7th-10th)

Stuyvesant Park Ball Fields
6th-12th St and FDR Drive

TriBeCa

Tribeca Dog Run
Warren St.
(Washington/West Side Hwy)

Union Square

Friends of Union Square Dog Run
SW Corner of Union Square
(13th/Broadway)

Dog Runs

Upper East Side

Carl Schurz Park - Gracie Square
East End Ave. (84th-89th St.)

East River Pavilion
York Ave. (@ 60th St.)
East River
212.755.3288

Upper West Side

Canine Court Van Courtland Park
W. 252nd St. (@ Broadway)

Central Park
Central Park W. - 5th Ave.
59th - 110th St.

Riverside Park
Riverside Drive
(@ 77th, 87th, 105th, 121st)

Theodore Roosevelt Park - Teddy's Dog Run
81st St. (@ Columbus Ave.)

West 23rd - 59th St.

DeWitt Clinton Park
Main run -52nd St. (@11th Ave.)
11th Ave. (@54th)

Hell's Kitchen Dog Run
10th Ave. (39th/40th)
212.736.4536

West Village

West Village D.O.G.
Gansevoort (West Side Hwy - Washington St.)
212.807.0093
www.wvdog.org

Washington Square Park - George's Run
W. 4th St.
(Thompson - McDougal)

East 23rd - 59th St.

Cohen's
108 E. 23rd St.
212.677.3707

Elite Optique
510 Madison Ave
212.421.1164

Gramercy Eyewear
240 3rd Ave
212.254.5535

H.L. Purdy, Inc.
501 Madison Ave
212.688.8050
sales@hlpurdy.com
www.hlpurdy.com

Qiora
535 Madison Ave
212.527.9933

Selima @ Barneys NY
600 Madison Ave.
212.833.2038

East Village

Selima Optique
84 E. 7th St.
212.260.2495

Myoptics
42 St. Mark's Pl.
212.533.1577

NoHo

Selima Showroom
450 W. 15th St., Suite 650
212.206.8913

NoLIta

Lunettes et Chocolat
25 Prince St.
212.334.8484
212.925.8800

SoHo

Niwaka
464 Broome St.
212.941.5410
www.niwaka.com

Selima Optique SoHo
59 Wooster St.
212.343.9490

TriBeCa

Worthy Eyes, Ltd.
40 Worth St. (@ Church St.)
212.233.2203

Upper East Side

H.L. Purdy, Inc.
971 Madison Ave
212.794.2509
sales@hlpurdy.com
www.hlpurdy.com

Upper East Side (cont'd)

H.L. Purdy, Inc.
1171 Madison Ave
212.249.3997
sales@hlpurdy.com
www.hlpurdy.com

H.L. Purdy, Inc.
1195 Madison Ave
212.737.0371
sales@hlpurdy.com
www.hlpurdy.com

Selima Optique Madison Avenue
899 Madison Ave.
212.988.6690

Upper West Side

Euro Optika
333 W. 57th St. (8th/9th)
212.262.5757

Upper West Side (cont'd)

Euro Optika
288 Columbus Ave(73rd/74th)
212.501.7070

Eye Q Optometrist
381 Amsterdam Ave.
212.724.8855
www.eyehoo.com

Ideal Eyes, Inc.
2301 Broadway
212.787.8477

Sun Goddess
473 Amsterdam Ave.
(82nd/83rd)
917.441.4141

The Eye Man, LTD
2264 Broadway (81st/82nd)
212.873.4114

West 23rd - 59th St.

Morganthal Fredrics
754 5th Ave.
Bergdorf Goodman (Plaza Lvl)
212.872.2526

West Village

Desiron
139 W. 22nd St.
212.414.4070
www.desiron.com

My Optics
96 7th Ave
212.633.6054

My Optics
82 Christopher St.
212.741.9550

Upper West Side

Gallery II Collections, Inc.
2244 Broadway
212.877.9780

LaBelle Epoque
280 Columbus Ave. (@ 73rd)
212.362.1770
posters@la-belle-epoque.com
www.la-belle-epoque.com

TriBeCa

1 Hour Flower.com
W. Broadway
800.958.0008
www.1hourflower.com

Anne/Bruno
115 W. Broadway
212.766.5660

SoHo

Belenky Brothers
151 Wooster St.
212.674.4242

Gallery 91
91 Grand St.
212.966.3722

Oprea Gallery
15 Spring St.
212.966.6675

Ward-Nasse Gallery
178 Prince St.
212.925.6951
www.wardnasse.org

Chelsea

La Maison Moderne
144 W. 19th St. (6th/7th)

East 23rd - 59th St.

Body Shop, The
509 Madison Ave
212.829.8603

Body Shop, The
Rockefeller Center

Body Shop, The
41st St. (@ 5th Ave.)

Crabtree & Evelyn, LTD.
520 Madison Ave
212.758.7847
www.crabtree-evelyn.com

Hides In Shape
555 Madison Ave
212.371.5998

East 23rd - 59th St. (cont'd)

Hides In Shape
630 3rd Ave.
212.661.2590

Paper Emporium
835A 2nd Ave
212.697.6573

Rebecca Moss, LTD
510 Madison Ave
212.832.7671

Staghorn, LTD
362 3rd Ave. (@ 26th St.)
212.832.2416

East Village

Body Shop, The
8th St. (@ Broadway)

Exit 9
64 Ave. A
212.228.0145

Flatiron

Aveda
140 5th Ave.
212.645.4797

Body Shop, The
20th St. (@ 5th Ave.)

NoLIta

Gates of Morocco, Inc.
8 Prince St.
212.925.2650

George Smith
73 Spring St.
212.226.4747

Kar'iter
19 Prince St.
212.274.1966

Lunettes et Chocolat
25 Prince St.
212.334.8484
212.925.8800

NoLIta (cont'd)

New York Firefighter's Friend
263 Lafayette St.
212.226.3142

SoHo

Aveda
233 Spring St.
212.807.1490

Aveda
456 W. Broadway
212.473.0280

Chimera
77 Mercer St.
212.334.4730

Framed on Prince
124 Prince St.
212.219.9040

Julian & Sara
103 Mercer St.
212.226.1989

SoHo (cont'd)

Prince & Sullivan 1 Hr Photo
186 Prince St.
212.941.0833

Quinto Sol
250 Lafayette St.
212.334.2255

TriBeCa

YHK
11 Jay St.(Hudson/Greenwich)
212.226.1300

Upper East Side

An American Craftsman
1222 2nd Ave.
212.794.3440

Upper East Side (cont'd)

Caron
675 Madison Ave
212.319.4888

Erwin Pearl
697 Madison Ave
212.753.3155
www.erwinpearl.com

Jacardi
787 Madison Ave. (@ 60th)
212.535.3200

Le Chien @ Trump Plaza
1044 3rd Ave. (@ 61st)
212.861.8100

Not Just For Dogs
244 E. 60th St. (2nd/3rd)

Spectra
903 Madison Ave.
212.744.2255

Upper West Side

Bath Island
69 Amsterdam Ave.
212.787.9415
bathisland@netscape.net
www.bathisland.com

Body Shop, The
76th St. (@ Broadway)

Cardeology
314 Columbus Ave.
(74th/75th)
212.579.9310

Cardeology
452 Amsterdam Ave.
(81st/82nd)
212.873.2491

Country Corner
196 Columbus Ave.

Laura Ashley, Inc.
398 Columbus Ave.
212.496.5110

Tibet Bazaar
473 Amsterdam Ave.
(82nd/83rd)
212.595.8487

West 23rd - 59th St.

An American Craftsman
60 W. 50th St.
212.586.3091

An American Craftsman
790 7th Ave.
212.399.2555

West Village

Charley and Kelley
353 Bleecker St.
212.414.0638

Details
347 Bleecker St. (@ 10th St.)
212.414.0039

DVVS
263A W. 19th St.
212.366.4888
www.dvvs.com

West Village (cont'd)

Enchanted Candle
22 Greenwich Ave.
212.924.1101
webmaster@enchantedcandle.com
www.enchantedcandle.com

Hudson Street Papers
357 Bleecker St.

Le Gamin
114 W. Houston St.
646.654.6685

London Boutique
85 Christopher St.
212.647.9106

Rainbows & Triangles
192 8th Ave.
212.627.2166

Roger & Dave
123 7th Ave.
212.989.1184

Roger & Dave
224 8th Ave.
212.645.4563

West Village (cont'd)

The Alternative
85 Christopher St.
212.645.8966

TriBeCa

**Ace of TriBeCa
Hardware**
160 W. Broadway
212.571.3788

All Areas

Door Store
www.doorstorefurniture.com

Chelsea

Bed, Bath & Beyond
6th Ave. (@ 17th St.)

La Maison Moderne
144 W. 19th St. (6th/7th)

New York Home
37 W. 17th St.
212.366.6880

East 23rd - 59th St.

Kama
368 3rd Ave.
212.689.7517

Staghorn, LTD
362 3rd Ave. (@ 26th St.)
212.832.2416

East 23rd - 59th St. (cont'd)

Simon's Hardware & Bath
421 3rd Ave.
212.532.9220

East Village

Exit 9
64 Ave. A
212.228.0145

Galleria J. Antonio
47 Ave. A
212.505.5512

NoLIta

Gates of Morocco, Inc
8 Prince St.
212.925.2650

NoLIta (cont'd)

ar'iter
9 Prince St.
12.274.1966

Modern Furniture asement
32 Crosby St.
12.334.9757

Rustika
3 Crosby St.
12.965.0004

SoHo

d Hoc
36 Wooster St.
12.982.7703

lice's Antiques
2 Greene St.

Modern
53 Wooster St.
12.253.0111

SoHo (cont'd)

Boca Grande
66 Greene St.
212.334.6120

Boffi SoHo
31 Greene St.
212.431.8282

Broadway Pan Handler
477 Broome St.

Coconut Company
131 Greene St.
212.539.1935

Craft Caravan Inc.
63 Greene St.
212.431.6669

Desiron
111 Greene St.
212.966.0404

Format
50 Wooster St.
212.941.7995
www.formatnyc.com

Jonathan Adler
465 Broome St.

SoHo (cont'd)

King's Road
42 Wooster
St(Grand/Broome)
212.941.5011
www.kingsroad.com

Paterae
458 Broome St.
212.941.0880

Portico
72 Spring St.
212.941.7800
www.porticohome.com

Quinto Sol
250 Lafayette St.
212.334.2255

Rabun & Claiborne
115 Crosby St.
212.226.5053

Roots
270 Lafayette St., Suite 1410
212.324.3333
www.roots.com

Rustika
63 Crosby St.
212.965.0004

SoHo (cont'd)

Sarajo
130 Greene St.
212.966.6156

Spazonavigl
113 Mercer St.
212.226.2364

Troy
138 Greene St.
212.941.4777

Val Cucine
152 Wooster St.
212.253.5969
www.valcucineny.com

Water Works
469 Broome St.
212.966.0605

TriBeCa

Antiqueria TriBeCa
129 Duane St.
212.227.7500
www.antiqueria.com

Home Furnishings

TriBeCa (cont'd)

Interieurs
149-151 Franklin St.
212.343.0800

John Kelly Furniture Design
7 Franklin St.
212.625.3355
kfurndsgn@aol.com

Totem
1 Franklin St.
212.925.5506

Urban Archaeology
143 Franklin St.
212.431.4646

Whimsy Blue
77 W. Broadway
212.941.8474
www.whimsyblue.com

White
5 White St.
212.964.4694
www.whiteonwhite.com

Union Square

ABC Carpet
881-888 Broadway
(@19th St.)
212.473.3000

Upper East Side

E. Braun & Co.
717 Madison Ave.
212.838.0650

Jacardi
787 Madison Ave. (@ 60th)
212.535.3200

Laytner's Linen & Home
237 E. 86th St.
212.996.4439

Upper West Side

Door Store
601 Amsterdam Ave.
212.501.8696

Upper West Side (cont'd)

Laura Ashley, Inc.
398 Columbus Ave.
212.496.5110

Laytner's
2270 Broadway (@ 81st)
212.724.0180
www.laytners.com

Metropolitan Design Center
2200 Broadway (@ 78th)
212.712.2258
212.712.2097

East 23rd - 59th St.

Four Seasons, The
7 E. 57th St.
www.fourseasons.com

Loews Hotel
69 Lexington Ave.
212.752.7000

Roger Williams, The
4 W. 44th St.
212.448.7000

Royalton Hotel
68 3rd Ave.
212.869.4400

St. Regis Hotel
E. 55th St.
212.753.4500

SoHo

SoHo Grand Hotel
10 W. Broadway
800.965.3000

SoHo (cont'd)

The Mercer
147 Mercer St.
212.966.6060

TriBeCa

TriBeCa Grand
2 6th Ave.
212.519.6600
www.tribecagrand.com

Upper East Side

Carlyle Hotel
35 E. 76th St.
212.744.1600

Franklin, The
164 E. 87th St. (@ Lexington)
212.369.1000

Hotel Plaza Athenee
37 E. 64th St. (Park/Madison)
212.734.9100

Upper East Side (cont'd)

Pierre
2 E. 61st St.
212.838.8000
Small dogs only, please.

Regency Hotel
540 Park Ave.
212.759.4100

Wales Hotel
1295 Madison Ave.
212.876.6000

West 23rd - 59th St.

Renaissance New York Hotel
714 7th Ave.
212.765.7676
Small & Medium dogs only

Mainsfield
12 W. 44th St.
212.944.6050

East 23rd - 59th St.

Cellini, NYC
509 Madison Ave.(@ 53rd St.)
212.888.0505

Links
535 Madison Ave.
212.588.1177
800.210.0079

Staghorn, LTD
362 3rd Ave. (@ 26th St.)
212.832.2416

Tiffany & Co.
525 5th Ave (@57th)

East Village

Galleria J. Antonio
37 Ave. A
212.505.5512

The Shape of Lies
127 E. 7th St.
212.533.5420

NoLIta

Dalidada
35 Spring St.
212.431.3285

SoHo

Belenky Brothers
151 Wooster St.
212.674.4242

Fragments
107 Greene St.
212.334.9588

Hanskoch
174 Prince St.
212.226.5385

Jack Spade
56 Greene St.
212.625.1820

Jill Platner
113 Crosby St.
212.324.1298
www.jillplatner.com

SoHo (cont'd)

Niwaka
464 Broome St.
212.941.5410
www.niwaka.com

SoHo Gem
367 W. Broadway
212.625.3004

Stuart Moore
128 Prince St.
212.941.1023

Swatch
438 W. Broadway
646.613.0160

The Joan Michlin Gallery
56 Greene St.
212.625.1820

Versani
152 Mercer St.
212.941.7770

Yvone Christa
107 Mercer St.
212.965.1001

Upper East Side

Alex Gordon Jewelers
1186 3rd Ave. (@ 69th)
212.570.6773

Alex Gordon Jewelers
1022 Madison Ave.
(78th/79th)
212.628.7915

David Yurman
780 Madison Ave.

Ilias Lalaounis
733 Madison Ave.
212.439.9400

Lanciani
826 Lexington Ave.
212.832.2092

Lanciani
992 Madison Ave.
212.717.2759

Liliblue
955 Madison Ave.
212.249.5356

Upper East Side (cont'd)

Manfredi
37 Madison Ave.
12.734.8710

Michael Ashton
33 Madison Ave. (@74th)
12.517.6655

SoHo Gem
80 Madison Ave.

Vertigo
55 Madison Ave.
12.439.9826

Zig Zag
63 Madison Ave.
12.472.6373

Zig Zag
336A 3rd Ave.
12.794.3178

Upper West Side

Alex Gordon Jewelers
328 Broadway (84th/85th)
12.724.8710

Upper West Side (cont'd)

Alex Gordon Jewelers
2230 Columbus Ave.
(70th/71st)
212.721.4368

Daphne
467 Amsterdam Ave.
212.877.5073
www.daphne1.com

Roslyn
276 Columbus Ave.
212.496.5050

Tibet Bazaar
473 Amsterdam Ave.
(82nd/83rd)
212.595.8487

West Village

Eastern Arts
365 Bleecker St.
212.929.7460

West Village (cont'd)

Charley and Kelley
353 Bleecker St.
212.414.0638

DVVS
263A W. 19th St.
212.366.4888
www.dvvs.com

Gallery Eclectic
43 Greenwich Ave.
212.924.4314

Graphic Village Wear
87 Christopher St.
212.929.0688

Yamak, Inc.
321 1/2 Bleecker St.
(Christopher/Grove)
212.807.9100

Chelsea

Chelsea Kids Quarters
33 W. 17th St. (5th/6th)
212.627.5524

East Village

Joanie James
117 E. 7th St.
212.505.9653

SoHo

Julian & Sara
103 Mercer St.
212.226.1989

Just For Tykes
83 Mercer St.
212.274.9121

Lilliput
240 Lafayette St.
212.965.9567
www.lilliputsoho.com

TriBeCa

BU and the Duck.com
106 Franklin St.
212.431.9226
www.buandtheduck.com

Shoo Fly
42 Hudson St.
212.406.3270
www.shoofly.com

Upper East Side

Bon Point
811 Madison Ave.
212.879.0900

Bon Point
1269 Madison Ave.
212.722.7720

Calypso
935 Madison Ave.
212.535.4100

Greenstones & CIE
442 Columbus Ave.
212.580.4322

Upper East Side (cont'd)

Loro Piana
821 Madison Ave.

Moschino
803 Madison Ave.
212.639.9600

Prince & Princess
33 E. 68th St.
212.879.8989

Upper West Side

Cradle & All
110 W. 86th St.
212.580.3801
www.cradleandallnyc.com

Granny Made
381 Amsterdam Ave.
(78th/79th)
212.496.1222
www.granny-made.com

Upper West Side (cont'd)

Greenstones & CIE
442 Columbus Ave.
212.580.4322

ShooFly
465 Amsterdam Ave.
212.580.4390

Tip Top Kids
149 W. 72nd St.
212.874.1004

Liquor Stores

East 23rd - 59th St.

D'vine Wines & Spirits
764 3rd Ave. (47th/48th)
212.317.1169

**Thomas J. McAdam
Liquor Co., Inc.**
398 3rd Ave.
212.683.3276
212.679.1224/5
www.mcadam-buyrite.com

West Village

Spirits of Carmine
52 Carmine St.
212.206.0091

All Areas

Coach
212.754.0041

Chelsea

Lambertson Truex.com
19 W. 21st St.
212.243.7671
www.lambertsontruex.com

East 23rd - 59th St.

Asprey & Garrard
725 5th Ave. (@ 56th St.)
212.688.1811

Body Shop, The
509 Madison Ave
212.829.8603

Body Shop, The
Rockefeller Center

East 23rd - 59th St. (cont'd)

Body Shop, The
41st St. (@ 5th Ave.)

Hides In Shape
555 Madison Ave
212.371.5998

Hides In Shape
630 3rd Ave.
212.661.2590

Kama
368 3rd Ave.
212.689.7517

Links
535 Madison Ave.
212.588.1177
800.210.0079

Prada
750 5th Ave. (56th/57th)
212.664.0010

Tumi
520 Madison Ave. (@ 54th)
212.813.0545

East Village

Body Shop, The
8th St. (@ Broadway)

Flatiron

Body Shop, The
20th St. (@ 5th Ave.)

SoHo

**Alexia Crawford
Accessories**
199 Prince St.
212.473.9703

f
94 Grand St.
212.334.4964

Jill Stuart
100 Greene St.
212.343.2300

SoHo (cont'd)

Jack Spade
56 Greene St.
212.625.1820

Monsac
339 Broadway
212.925.3237
www.monsac.com

Men's Accessories

Pastel
459 Broome St.
212.219.3922

Upper East Side

Bottega Veneta
655 Madison Ave
212.371.5511

Upper East Side (cont'd)

Calypso
935 Madison Ave.
212.535.4100

Emporio Armani
601 Madison Ave.
212.317.0800

Ilias Lalaounis
733 Madison Ave.
212.439.9400

Krizia
769 Madison Ave
212.879.1211

L'Occitane
Madison Ave. (@ 80th St.)
212.355.6135

Lana Marks
645 Madison Ave
212.355.6135

Prada
841 Madison Ave (@70th)
212.327.4200

Upper East Side (cont'd)

Roberto Cavalli
711 Madison Ave.

Robert Cler Gerie
681 Madison Ave.
212.207.8600

Scully & Scully Park Ave.
504 Park Ave. (59th/60th)
212.327.4200

Sergio Rossi
835 Madison Ave.
212.396.4814

Stephane Kelian
717 Madison Ave.
212.980.1919

Valentino
747 Madison Ave.
212.772.6969

Upper West Side

Bath Island
469 Amsterdam Ave.
212.787.9415
bathisland@netscape.net
www.bathisland.com

Upper West Side (cont'd)

Body Shop, The
76th St. (@ Broadway)

Roslyn
276 Columbus Ave.
212.496.5050

Tano
2286 Broadway (82nd/83rd)
212.362.5070

Tibet Bazaar
473 Amsterdam Ave.
(82nd/83rd)
212.595.8487

West 23rd - 59th St.

Hermes
11 E. 57th St. (6th/7th)
212.751.3181

Prada
750 5th Ave. (56th/57th)
212.664.0010

West Village

Graphic Village Wear
87 Christopher St.
212.929.0688

Chelsea

Gerry's Menswear
110 8th Ave.
212.243.9141

East 23rd - 59th St.

Club Monaco
55th St. (@ 5th Ave)
646.497.1116

H. Herzfeld, Inc.
507 Madison Ave
212.753.6756
www.herzfeldonline.com

Kama
368 3rd Ave.
212.689.7517

Prada
750 5th Ave. (56th/57th)
212.664.0010

Saks 5th Ave.
611 5th Ave. (@ 50th)
212.753.4000

East 23rd - 59th St. (cont'd)

Vintage Thrift Shop, The
286 3rd Ave. (22nd/23rd)
212.871.0777

East Village

Garosparo
119 St. Mark's Pl.
(1st/Ave. A)
212.533.7835

Flatiron

Club Monaco
21st St. (@ 5th Ave.)
212.352.0936

NoHo

Nylon Squid
222 Lafayette St.
212.334.6554

NoLIta

Inhumane Shop
195 Mulberry St.
212.331.0499

Ina Men
262 Mott St.
212.334.2210

Minlee
7 Prince St.
212.334.6978

Nylon Squid
222 Lafayette St.
212.334.6554

X-Large
267 Lafayette St.
212.334.4480

SoHo

Afterlife
59 Greene St.
212.625.3167

A.P.C.
131 Mercer St.
212.966.9685

Club Monaco
Prince St.
646.533.8930

Helmut Lange
80 Greene St.
212.925.7214

Hugo Boss
132 Greene St.
212.965.1300

John Varuatos
149 Mercer St.
212.965.0700

Joseph
106 Greene St.
212.343.7071

Lucky Brand Jeans
38 Greene St.
212.625.0707

SoHo (cont'd)

Malo
125 Wooster St.

Mare
426 W. Broadway
212.343.1110

Onward
172 Mercer St.
212.274.1255

Phat Farm
129 Prince St.
212.533.7428

Quicksilver
109-111 Spring St.
212.334.4500

R by 45 rpm
169 Mercer St.
917.237.0045

Replay
109 Prince St.
212.673.6300

Rugby North America
115 Mercer St.
212.431.3069

SoHo (cont'd)

Stussy NYC
140 Wooster St.
212.995.8787

Ted Baker NYC
107 Grand St.
212.343.8989

Yohji Yamamoto USA
103 Grand St.
212.966.9066

Yves Saint Laurent
88 Wooster St.
212.274.0522

TriBeCa

Detour
425-475 W. Broadway
212.625.1820

Mare
426 W. Broadway
212.343.1110

Union Square

Emporio Armani
110 5th Ave.
212.727.3240

Paul Smith
108 5th Ave. (@ 16th)
212.627.9770

Upper East Side

Barney's New York
Madison Ave. at 61st St.
212.826.8900

Bergdorf Goodman
754 5th Ave. (@58th St.)
212.753.7300

Bloomingdale's
1000 3rd Ave. (59th/60th)
212.705.2000

Bottega Veneta
655 Madison Ave
212.371.5511

Upper East Side (cont'd)

Burberry London
9 E. 57th St. (Madison/5th)
212.371.5010

Calypso
935 Madison Ave.
212.535.4100

Cerruti
789 Madison Ave.
212.327.2222

Club Monaco
65th St. (@ 3rd Ave.)
646.533.8930

DKNY
655 Madison Ave. (@60th St.)
212.223.3569

Emporio Armani
601 Madison Ave.
212.317.0800

Gia Franco Ferre
845 Madison Ave.
212.717.5430

Upper East Side (cont'd)

Gianni Versace
815 Madison Ave.
212.744.6868

Gucci
685 5th Ave. (@54th)
212.826.2600

Issey Miyake
992 Madison Ave.
212.439.7822
madison@isseymiyake.com

Krizia
769 Madison Ave
212.879.1211

Michael Kors
974 Madison Ave.
212.452.4685

Moschino
803 Madison Ave.
212.639.9600

Robert Marc
782 Madison Ave.
212.737.6000

Upper East Side (cont'd)

Robert Marc
1046 Madison Ave.
212.988.9600

Robert Marc
1300 Madison Ave.
212.722.1600

Roberto Cavalli
711 Madison Ave.

Super Runners Shop
1246 3rd Ave.
212.249.2133

Super Runners Shop
1337 Lexington Ave.
212.369.6010

Tse
827 Madison Ave.
212.472.7790

Valentino
747 Madison Ave.
212.772.6969

Versace
815 Madison Ave.
212.744.6868

Upper West Side

Bath Island
469 Amsterdam Ave.
212.787.9415
bathisland@netscape.net
www.bathisland.com

Club Monaco
2376 Broadway
212.579.2587

Frank Stella Clothiers
440 Columbus Ave. (@ 81st)
646.877.5566

Granny Made
381 Amsterdam Ave.
(78th/79th)
212.496.1222
www.granny-made.com

Super Runners Shop
360 Amsterdam Ave.
212.787.7665

Tibet Bazaar
473 Amsterdam Ave.
(82nd/83rd)
212.595.8487

West 23rd - 59th St.

Frank Stella Clothiers
921 7th Ave. (@ 58th St.)
646.957.1600

Hermes
11 E. 57th St. (6th/7th)
212.751.3181

West Village

Fashion Storm, Inc.
306 Bleecker St.
212.414.4080

Gerry's Menswear
110 8th Ave.
212.243.9141

Gerry's Menswear
353 Bleecker St.
212.243.9233

Graphic Village Wear
87 Christopher St.
212.929.0688

West Village (cont'd)

Loft
89 Christopher St.
212.691.2334

L'Uomo
383 Bleecker St.
212.206.1844

Marc Jacobs
403 Bleecker St.
212.924.0026

Starting Line, The
180 8th Ave.
212.691.4729

World
222 8th Ave.
212.206.8880

World
75 Christopher St.
212.675.1364

East Village

Etherea
56 Ave. A
212.358.1126

Kim's Video & Music
6 St. Mark's Pl.
212.598.9985

West Village

Bleecker St. Records
239 Bleecker St.
212.255.7899

Kim's Video & Music
144 Bleecker St.
212.387.8250
info@kimsvideo.com

Kim's Video & Music
350 Bleecker St.
212.675.8996
info@kimsvideo.com

London Boutique
35 Christopher St.
212.647.9106

Upper East Side

Morganthal Fredrics
699 Madison Ave.
212.838.3090

Upper West Side

Eye Q Optometrist
381 Amsterdam Ave.
212.724.8855
www.eyehoo.com

Central Park

Alice in Wonderland
E. 74th St.
North of Conservatory Water

Belvedere Castle
Mid-Park (79th/80th)
11am - 4pm Wed - Mon

Bethesda Terrace
Mid-Park (@ 72nd St.)

Carousel
Mid-Park (@ 64th St.)

Dog Hill (Cedar Hill)
East-Side Park (76th-79th)

George Delacorte Musical Clock
East-Side Park (63rd-66th)

The Great Hill
West-Side Park (103rd-107th)

Harlem Meer Loch
West-Side Park (100th-103rd)

Loeb Boat House & Lake
Boat House - East (74th/75th)
Lake - Mid-Park (71st-78th)

Central Park (cont'd)

Model Boat Pond, Conservatory Water
East-Side (72nd-75th)

The Ramble
Mid-Park (73rd-79th)

Ravine
Mid-Park (102nd-106th)

Reservoir
Mid-Park (85th-96th)

Scholars Walk
East-Side (@ 59th St.)

Shakespeare Garden
Mid-Park (@ 79th St.)

Strawberry Fields
72nd St & Central Park West

Zoo
East-Side (@ 59th)

East 23rd - 59th St.

St. Vartan's Park
1st Ave. (35th -36th)

Sutton Place Park
Sutton Place S. (54th - 57th)

TriBeCa

Duane Park
Intersection Duane/Hudson

James J. Walker Park
Hudson (Clarkson/Leroy)

Upper East Side

Carl Schurz Park
Gracie Square (84th/89th)

Conservatory Garden
105th St. (@ 5th Ave.)
8:00 am to dusk daily

Upper West Side

Dante Park
Lincoln Center
(65th/Columbus)

Edgar Allan Poe St.
84th St.
(Riverside - Broadway)

Park & Garden, Garden
55-57 W. 87th St.
(Central Park W. - Columbus)

Riverside Park
Riverside Dr.
(W. 72nd - 158th)

West End Towers Park
75 West End Ave. (63rd/64th)

West 23rd - 59th St.

Bryant Park
Avenue of the Americas
(40th - 42nd)

West 23rd - 59th St. (cont'd)

Clinton Community Garden
436 W. 48th St. (9th/10th)

West Village

Christopher Park
Sheridan Sq. (Christopher - Grove @ 7th Ave.)

Washington Square Park
W. 4th St.
(Thompson - McDougal)

All Areas

Michael Catron
646.331.7769

Petland Discounts
Over 100 locations

Chelsea

Andrea Arden Dog Training
212.213.4288

Bonnie's K9 Corp.
136 9th Ave.
212.414.2500
www.k9-swimtherapy.copy

City Dogs Obedience School
158 W. 23rd St. (6th/7th)
212.255.3618

Heart of Chelsea Animal Hospital
257 W. 18th St.
212.924.6116

Chelsea (cont'd)

New York Dog Spa & Hotel
145 W. 18th St. (6th/7th)
212.243.1199

Pet Parade LTD., The
144 W. 19th St.
212.645.5345
www.thepetparadeltd.com

East 23rd - 59th St.

Andrea Arden Dog Training
212.213.4288

Biscuits & Bath
227 E. 44th St.
212.692.2324

Doggie Do (and Pussycats Too!)
567 3rd Ave (37th/38th)
212.661.9111

Pet Supplies & Services

East 23rd - 59th St. (cont'd)

Natural Pet, The
238 3rd Ave.
212.228.4848

Prada
750 5th Ave. (56th/57th)
212.664.0010

Saks 5th Ave.
611 5th Ave. (@ 50th)
212.753.4000

Two Dogs & A Goat!
326 E. 34th St.
212.213.6979

East Village

Animal Crackers
26 1st Ave.
212.614.6786

Mikey's Pet Shop, Inc.
130 E 7th St.
212.477.3235

SoHo

Alternative Pet Care
33 Howard St.
212.941.5083

Fetch
43 Greenwich Ave. (6th/7th)
212.352.8591

Frenchware
98 Thompson St.
(Prince/Spring)
212.625.3131

Monsac (dog accessories)
339 W. Broadway
www.monsac.com

The Dog Wash
Grooming
177 MacDougal

The Pet Bar
311 E. 60th St.
212.355.2850
www.suttonpets.com

TriBeCa

Another Barking Zoo
368 1/2 Greenwich St.
(Franklin/N. Moore)
212.233.0226

Beasty Feast
650 Hudson (@ Jane)
212.620.7099

Wagging Tail, The
354 1/2 Greenwich St.
212.285.4900

Union Square

Paul Smith
108 5th Ave. (@ 16th)
212.627.9770

Upper West Side

Amsterdog Groomers
586 Amsterdam (88th/89th)
212.496.6117

Animal General
558 Columbus Ave.
212.501.9600

Upper West Side (cont'd)

Follow My Lead Dog Training
117 W. 74th St.
212.873.5511

Pet Bowl
440 Amsterdam (@ 81st)
212.595.4200

Pet Market, The
210 W. 72nd St.
(Broadway/West End Ave.)
212.799.4200

Pet Shop
564 Columbus Ave.
212.580.2400

West Village

American Dog Trainers Network
161 W. 4th St. (5th/6th)

Pet Supplies & Services

West Village (cont'd)

Beasty Feast
630 Hudson St. (@ Jane St.)
212.620.7099

Beasty Feast
237 Bleecker St. (@ 6th Ave.)
212.243.3261

Beasty Feast
680 Washington St.
(@ Charles St.)
212.620.4055

Beverly Hills Launder Mutt
45 Grove St.
212.691.7700

Bonnie's K-9 Swim Center
136 9th Ave. (18th/19th)
212.414.2500

Fetch
43 Greenwich Ave.
212.352.8591

Four Paws Club, The
387 Bleecker St.
212.367.8265

West Village (cont'd)

Groom-O-Rama, Inc.
496 6th Ave (12th/13th)
212.627.2899

Heart of Chelsea Animal Hospital
257 W. 18th St.
212.924.6116

New York Bed & Biscuit
5th Ave (@ Washington Sq.)
212.475.6064

Poodle Cut, The
14 Bedford St.
212.929.0137

Urban Bird
19 Greenwich St.
212.352.3332
www.urbanbird.com

Urban Pets
18 Christopher St.
212.828.4254

SoHo

Daniel Stein
500B Grand St.
212.388.1095

Prince & Sullivan 1Hr. Photo
186 Prince St.
212.941.0833

TriBeCa

DPI Photo Lab
87 Franklin St.
212.966.3485

Upper West Side

Spectra Photo/Digital
451 Amsterdam
212.362.0094
spectranyc@earthlink.net
www.spectra-nyc.com

West Village

Taranto Labs
245 W. 19th St.
212.691.6070
ken@tarantolab.com

Real Estate

All Areas

Douglas Elliman
212.650.4800

Halstead Property Group
1 W. Broadway
212.475.4200

Rezanamazi Real Estate
www.rezanamazirealestate.com

Chelsea

Fenwick-Keats Downtown, LLC
101 W. 11th St.
212.352.8144

SoHo

The Halstead Property Company
451 W. Broadway
212.475.4200

Upper East Side

Douglas Elliman
980 Madison Ave.
212.650.4800
www.douglaselliman.com

Fenwick-Keats Downtown, LLC
1185 Lexington Ave. (@80th)

Upper West Side

The Corcoran Group
2253 Broadway
212.875.2979
www.corcoran.com

West Village

Roomates, NYC
268 W. 22nd St.
212.627.1871
www.roomates-nyc.com

Chelsea

Cafeteria
119 7th Ave. (@ 17t St.)
212.414.1717

Chelsea Grill
135 8th Ave. (16th/17th)
212.255.3618

Chelsea Lobster Company
156 7th Ave. (@ 19th St.)
212.243.5732

Le Singe Vert
160 7th Ave. (19th/20th)
212.366.4100

Merchant's
112 7th Ave.

Paul & Jimmy's Ristorante
123 E. 18th St.
212.475.9540

Petite Abeille
107 W. 18th St. (6th/7th)
212.604.9350

Chelsea (cont'd)

Raymond's Cafe
88 7th Ave. (15th/16th)
212.929.1778

Restivo Ristorante
209 7th Ave. (@ 22nd St.)
212.366.4133

East 23rd - 59th St.

Cafe De Paris
924 2nd Ave. (@ 49th St.)
212.486.1411

Cafe St. Bart's
109 E. 50th St. (@ Park)
212.888.2664

Christina's
606 2nd Ave. (33rd/34th)
212.889.5169

Cinema
2 E. 45th St.
212.949.0600
www.cinemarestaurants.com

East 23rd - 59th St. (cont'd)

Cinema
505 3rd Ave.
212.689.9022
www.cinemarestaurants.com

Friend Of A Farmer
77 Irving Pl.
212.477.2188

San Pietro
18 E. 54th St.
212.753.9015
www.sanpietro.net

Typhoon
22 E. 54th St.
212.754.9006

East Village

Aunt B's on B
186 Ave. B. (11th/12th)
212.505.2071

East Village (cont'd)

Black-Eyed Suzie's Organic
128 E 7th St. (1st/Ave. A)
212.388.0707

Cafe Margaux
175 Ave. B (@ 11th St.)
212.260.7960

Casimir
103 Ave. B. (6th/7th)
212.995.5991

Crooked Tree Creperie
110 St. Mark's Pl.
(1st/Ave. A)
212.533.3299

Life Cafe
343 E. 10th St. (off Ave. B)
212.477.8791
www.lifecafenyc.com

La Gould Finch
93 Ave. B (@ 6th St.)
212.253.6369

Mesapotamia
98 Ave. B. (6th/7th)
212.358.1166

East Village (cont'd)

Ovo
65 2nd Ave. (3rd/4th)
212.353.1444

Pierrot Bistro
28 Ave. B (2nd/3rd)
212.673.1999

Pisces
95 Ave. A (@ 6th St.)
212.260.6660

Telephone Bar & Grill
149 2nd Ave. (9th/10th)
212.529.5000

Flatiron

Dano Restaurant & Bar
254 5th Ave. (27th/28th)
212.725.2922

SoHo

Bistro Le Amis
180 Spring St. (@ Thompson
212.226.8645

Bubby's Restaurant Bar & Bakery
120 Hudson St.
212.219.0666

Cub Room Cafe
131 Sullivan St. (@ Prince)
212.677.4100

Grey Dog's Coffee
33 Carmine St.
(Bleecker/Bedford)
212.462.0041

Once Upon A Tart
135 Sullivan St.
(Houston/Prince)
212.387.8869

Raoul's
180 Prince St.
(Sullivan/Thompson)
212.966.3518

SoHo Grand Hotel - Grand Bar
310 W. Broadway (@ Grand)
212.965.3000

SoHo (cont'd)

Space Untitled
133 Greene St.
(Houston/Prince)
212.260.8962

TriBeCa

Bassets Coffee & Tea
23 W. Broadway (@ Duane)
212.349.1662

Felix
340 W. Broadway (@ Grand)
212.431.0021

277 Church St.
212.625.0505

JA
01 Church St.

Le Pescadou
8 King St. (@6th Ave.)
212.924.3434

Union Square

The Coffee Shop
29 Union Square (@ 16th)
212.243.7969

Silver Swan
41 E. 20th St
(B'wy/Park Ave. S.)
212.254.3611

Verbena
54 Irving Place (17th/18th)
212.260.5454

Zen Palate
34 Union Square E. (@ 16th)
212.614.9291

Upper East Side

Atlantic Grill
1431 3rd Ave.
212.988.9200

Baraonda
1439 2nd Ave. (@ 74th)
212.288.8555

Upper East Side (cont'd)

Barking Dog Luncheonette
1678 3rd Ave. (@ 94th)
212.831.1800

Bistro du Nord
1312 Madison Ave. (@ 93rd)
212.289.0997

Cafe Nosidam
768 Madison Ave. (@ 66th)
212.717.5633

Cinema
1325 2nd Ave.
212.772.6400
www.cinemarestaurants.com

Ciao Bella Cafe
27 E. 92nd St. (5th/Madison)
212.831.5555

Coconut Grill
1481 2nd Ave.
212.772.6262

Ferrier
29 E. 65th St. (off Madison)
212.772.9000

Upper East Side (cont'd)

Ice Cream Cafe
Central Park (72nd/5th Ave.)

Leaping Frog Cafe
830 5th Ave. (@ 64th St.)
212.717.8918

Le Petit Hulot
973 Lexington Ave.(70th/71st)
212.794.9800

Merchant's
1125 1st Ave.

Merchant's
1608 1st Ave.

Park View at the Boathouse
Central Pk (72nd/E.Park Dr.N)
212.517.2233

Pascalou
1308 Madison Ave(92nd/93rd)
212.534.7522

Vespa Cibobuono
1625 2nd Ave (84th/85th)
212.472.2050

Upper East Side (cont'd)

Zocalo
174 E. 82nd St. (3rd/Lex)
212.717.7772

Upper West Side

Artie's New York
290 Broadway (82nd/83rd)
212.579.5959

Avenue
520 Columbus Ave.
212.579.3194

Bella Luna
584 Columbus Ave.
(@ 89th St.)
212.877.2267

Boulevard
2398 Broadway (@ 88th St.)
212.874.7400

Cafe Mozart
154 W. 70th St.
(@ Broadway)
212.595.9797

Upper West Side (cont'd)

Columbus Cafe
556 Columbus Ave.
(86th/87th)
212.721.9040

Firehouse
522 Columbus Ave.
(85th/86th)
212.787.3473

Fountain Cafe
Lincoln Center
(65th/Columbus)
212.874.7000

Isabella's
359 Columbus Ave.
212.724.2100

Josephina
1900 Broadway (63rd/64th)
212.799.1000

Merchant's
521 Columbus Ave. (@ 85th)
212.721.3689

Upper West Side (cont'd)

Metisse
239 W. 105th St.
(Amsterdam/Broadway)
212.666.8825

Mineral Springs Cafe
Central Park (70th@West Dr.)

North West
392 Columbus Ave.
212.799.4530

Ocean Grill
384 Columbus Ave.
212.579.2300

Opera Espresso Cafe
1928 Broadway (64th/65th)
212.799.3050

Pappardella
316 Columbus Ave.
212.595.7996

Tavern On The Green
Central Park West (66th/67th)
212.873.3200

West 23rd - 59th St.

Brasserie Centrale
1700 Broadway (@ 53rd)
212.757.2233

Bryant Park Cafe
25 W. 40th St.
(@ Ave. of the Americas)
212.840.6500

Puttanesca
859 9th Ave. (@56th)
212.581.4177

Rue 57
60 W. 57th St.
(@ Ave. of the Americas)
212.307.5656

Seppi's
123 W. 56th St. (6th/7th)
212.708.7444

West Village

Antonio
140 W. 13th St. (6th/7th)
212.645.4606

West Village (cont'd)

Arte
21 E. 9th St. (5th/University)
212.473.0077

Arte Pasta
81 Greenwich Ave. (Bank/7th)
212.229.0234

Bandito
33 Greenwich Ave.
212.807.0120

Bar Six
502 6th Ave. (12th/13th)
212.691.1363

Cafe San Marco
211 Waverly Pl. (7th/Charles)
212.367.7535

Chez Ma Tante
189 W. 10th St.
(Bleecker/7th)
212.620.0223

Cowgirl Hall of Fame
519 Hudson St. (@ 10th St.)
212.633.1133

West Village (cont'd)

Cuisine de Saigon
154 W. 13th St. (6th/7th)
212.255.6003

Da Silvano
260 6th Ave.
(Bleecker/Houston)
212.982.2343

Dew Drop Inn
57 Greenwich Ave.
212.924.8055

French Roast
78 W. 11th St. (@ 6th Ave.)
212.533.2233

Greenwich Street Cafe
75 Greenwich Ave.
(@ 7th Ave.)
212.255.5450

LeGans
842 Greenwich St.
212.675.5224

Les Deux Gamins
170 Waverly Pl. (@ Grove St.)
212.807.7357

West Village (cont'd)

Markt
401 W. 14th St. (@ 9th Ave.)
212.727.3314

Magnolio Bakery
401 Bleecker St. (@ 11th St.)
212.462.2572

Pastis
9 Ninth Ave.
(@ Little W. 12th St.)
212.929.4844

Philip Marie
569 Hudson St. (@ W. 11th)
212.242.6200

Salam Cafe & Restaurant
104 W. 13th St. (6th/7th)
212.741.0277

Sapore
55 Greenwich St.
212.229.0551

Sud
210 W. 10th St.
(Bleecker/W. 4th)
212.255.3805

West Village (cont'd)

Tartine
253 W. 11th St. (@ W. 4th)
212.229.2611

SoHo

Nomad Rugs
470 Broome St.
212.219.3330

NoLIta

Enve Salon
109 Crosby St.
212.334.3683

West Village

Mario Nico
266 W. 22nd St.
212.727.8464

Chelsea

Man's Fashionable Shoes
196 1/2 7th Ave. (21st/22nd)
212.675.0718

Medici
24 W. 23rd St. (5th/6th)
212.604.0888
mediciinc@msn.com

Sacco
94 7th Ave. (@ 16th)
212.675.5180
www.saccoshoes.com

East 23rd - 59th St.

Fratelli Rossetti
625 Madison Ave.
212.888.5107

Johnston & Murphy
345 Madison Ave.

East 23rd - 59th St. (cont'd)

Johnston & Murphy
520 Madison Ave.

Maraolo
782 Lexington Ave.
212.832.8182

Maraolo
551 Madison Ave.
212.308.8794

Maraolo
835 Madison Ave.
212.628.5080

East Village

Profiles
30 3rd Ave.
212.979.9724
siriam@webtv.net

Flatiron

Medici
309 5th Ave. (@ 32nd St.)
212.725.8798

NoLIta

Shoe
197 Mulberry St.
212.941.0205

Sigerson Morrison
28 Prince St.
212.219.3893

SoHo

Camper
125 Prince St.

Cowboy Boot Shoe Repair
4 Prince St.(4 blks E. of B'wy)
212.941.9532

SoHo (cont'd)

Jenny B.
118 Spring St.
212.343.9575

John Fluevog Shoes Ltd.
250 Mulberry St.

Kate Spade
454 Broome St.
212.274.1991

Kerquelen
44 Greene St.
212.431.1771
www.kerquelen.com

Kerquelen
430 W. Broadway
212.226.8313
www.kerquelen.com

Nancy Geist
107 Spring St.
212.925.7192

Prada
750 5th. Ave (56th/57th)
212.664.0010

SoHo (cont'd)

Sacco
111 Thompson St.
212.925.8010
www.saccoshoes.com

Stephanie Kelian
158 Mercer St.
212.925.3077

Upper East Side

Bati
105L 3rd Ave. (62nd/63rd)

Bottega Veneta
555 Madison Ave
212.371.5511

Maraolo
1321 3rd Ave
212.535.6225

Prada
841 Madison Ave (@70th)
212.327.4200

Upper East Side (cont'd)

Rapax
1100 Madison Ave
212.734.5171

Roberto Cavalli
711 Madison Ave.

Robert Cler Gerie
681 Madison Ave.
212.207.8600

Sergio Rossi
835 Madison Ave.
212.396.4814

Stephane Kelian
717 Madison Ave.
212.980.1919

Stuart Weitzman
625 Madison Ave
212.750.2555

Super Runners Shop
1246 3rd Ave.
212.249.2133

Super Runners Shop
1337 Lexington Ave.
212.369.6010

Upper East Side (cont'd)

Via Spiga
765 Madison Ave.
212.988.4877

Upper West Side

Bati
2323 Broadway (84th/85th)
212.724.7214

Montmartre
2212 Broadway
212.875.8430

Montmartre
247 Columbus Ave.
212.721.7760

Profiles
294 Columbus Ave. (@ 74th)
212.799.1994
siriam@webtv.net

Upper West Side (cont'd)

Sacco
2355 Broadway (@ 86th)
212.874.8362
www.saccoshoes.com

Sacco
324 Columbus Ave.
212.799.5229
www.saccoshoes.com

Steve Madden
2315 Broadway
212.799.4221
www.stevemadden.com

Super Runners Shop
360 Amsterdam Ave.
212.787.7665

Tani
131 W. 72nd St.
212.595.1338
www.tanishoes.com

Tano
2286 Broadway (82nd/83rd)
212.362.5070

West Village

London Boutique
85 Christopher St.
212.647.9106

Telephone Supplies & Services

East 23rd - 59th St.

Mobile City
575 5th Ave.

Mobile City
575 Madison Ave.

Personal Communication Center
220 3rd Ave.
212.253.0800

Wireless Concepts
489 3rd Ave.
212.679.6077
msrlinks@aol.com

TriBeCa

In Touch Wireless
303 Greenwich St.
212.587.0007

Wireless Warehouse
200 Church St.
212.619.1000

Union Square

Totally Connected
111 3rd Ave (@ 14th St.)
212.539.9999

Upper East Side

Totally Connected
352 E. 86th St.
212.794.5200

Upper West Side

Wireless Solutions
324 Columbus Ave.
(75th/76th)
212.496.9515

West 23rd - 59th St.

Mobile City
299 Broadway
212.385.5353

West 23rd - 59th St. (cont'd)

Mobile City
526 7th Ave.

Mobile City
1230 6th Ave.

West Village

Z Wireless
50 Greenwich Ave.
212.647.0212

All Areas

Hampton Jitney
800.936.0440
All dogs must be in carrier.
Small dogs only.

Hampton Limo
800.936.0440
Press #5

Long Island Railroad
Penn Station
34th St./7th Ave.
718.217.5477

New York Water Taxi
212.681.8111

East Village

Kim's Video & Music
6 St. Mark's Pl.
212.505.0311

West Village

Kim's Video & Music
144 Bleecker St.
212.260.1010
info@kimsvideo.com

Kim's Video & Music
350 Bleecker St.
212.675.8996
info@kimsvideo.com

London Boutique
35 Christopher St.
212.647.9106

World of Video
510 Greenwich Ave.
212.627.1095

Chelsea

Lambertson Truex.com
19 W. 21st St.
212.243.7671
www.lambertsontruex.com

East 23rd - 59th St.

Body Shop, The
509 Madison Ave
212.829.8603

Body Shop, The
Rockefeller Center

Body Shop, The
41st St. (@ 5th Ave.)

Hides In Shape
555 Madison Ave
212.371.5998

Hides In Shape
630 3rd Ave.
212.661.2590

East 23rd - 59th St. (cont'd)

Kama
368 3rd Ave.
212.689.7517

Links
535 Madison Ave.
212.588.1177
800.210.0079

Michel's Bags
672 Lexington Ave(55th/56th)
212.872.1320

Michel's Bags
510 Madison Ave.(52nd/53rd)
212.355.8309

Prada
750 5th Ave. (56th/57th)
212.664.0010

Tumi
520 Madison Ave. (@ 54th)
212.813.0545

Zan Boutique
810 2nd Ave. (@ 43rd St.)
212.687.3304

East Village

Body Shop, The
8th St. (@ Broadway)

Flatiron

Body Shop, The
20th St. (@ 5th Ave.)

NoLIta

ASP
185 Mulberry St.
212.431.1682

SoHo

Furla
430 Broadway
212.343.0048

SoHo (cont'd)

Kate Spade
454 Broome St.

Monsac
339 Broadway
212.925.3237
www.monsac.com

Yvone Christa
107 Mercer St.
212.965.1001
www.yvonechrista.com

Upper East Side

Bebe
1044 Madison Ave.
212.517.2323

Bebe
1127 3rd Ave.
212.935.2444

Bottega Veneta
655 Madison Ave
212.371.5511

Upper East Side (cont'd)

Calypso
935 Madison Ave.
212.535.4100

Celine
667 Madison Ave.
212.486.9700

Emporio Armani
601 Madison Ave.
212.317.0800

Furla
727 Madison Ave.
212.755.8986

Genny
831 Madison Ave.
212.249.9660

Ilias Lalaounis
733 Madison Ave.
212.439.9400

Krizia
769 Madison Ave
212.879.1211

Upper East Side (cont'd)

Lana Marks
645 Madison Ave
212.355.6135

Loro Piana
821 Madison Ave.

Prada
841 Madison Ave (@70th)
212.327.4200

Roberto Cavalli
711 Madison Ave.

Robert Cler Gerie
681 Madison Ave.
212.207.8600

Scully & Scully Park Ave.
504 Park Ave. (59th/60th)
212.327.4200

Sergio Rossi
835 Madison Ave.
212.396.4814

Sonia Rykiel
849 Madison Ave.
212.396.3060

Upper East Side (cont'd)

Stephane Kelian
717 Madison Ave.
212.980.1919

Via Spiga
765 Madison Ave.
212.988.4877

Wolford
619 Madison Ave. (@ 77th)
212.688.4850

Worldly Things
837 Madison Ave.
212.988.7810

Upper West Side

Bath Island
469 Amsterdam Ave.
212.787.9415
bathisland@netscape.net
www.bathisland.com

Upper West Side (cont'd)

Body Shop, The
76th St. (@ Broadway)

Laura Ashley, Inc.
398 Columbus Ave.
212.496.5110

Liana
324 Columbus Ave.
(75th/76th)
212.873.8746

Montmartre
2212 Broadway
212.875.8430

Montmartre
247 Columbus Ave.
212.721.7760

Off Broadway Boutique
139 W. 72nd St.
212.724.6713

Really Great Things
284A Columbus Ave.
212.787.5354

Upper West Side (cont'd)

Roslyn
276 Columbus Ave.
212.496.5050

Tibet Bazaar
473 Amsterdam Ave.
(82nd/83rd)
212.595.8487

Zan Boutique
2394 Broadway
212.877.4853

West 23rd - 59th St.

Hermes
11 E. 57th St. (6th/7th)
212.751.3181

Prada
750 5th Ave. (56th/57th)
212.664.0010

Zan Boutique
1666 Broadway (51st/52nd)
212.582.5580

West Village

Yamak, Inc.
321 1/2 Bleecker St.
(Christopher/Grove)
212.807.9100

Women's Clothes

East 23rd - 59th St.

Club Monaco
55th St. (@ 5th Ave)
646.497.1116

Eileen Fisher
521 Madison Ave.
212.759.9888

Fogal
510 Madison Ave.
info@fogal.com

Kama
368 3rd Ave.
212.689.7517

Prada
750 5th Ave. (56th/57th)
212.664.0010

Saks 5th Ave.
611 5th Ave. (@ 50th)
212.753.4000

Vintage Thrift Shop, The
286 3rd Ave. (22nd/23rd)
212.871.0777

East 23rd - 59th St. (cont'd)

Zan Boutique
810 2nd Ave. (@ 43rd St.)
212.687.3304

East Village

Cherry Bishop Clothing
117-119 E. 7th St.
212.529.4608

Garosparo
119 St. Mark's Pl.
(1st/Ave. A)
212.533.7835

Mode
109 St. Mark's Pl.
212.529.9208

Mo Mo Fa Lana
43 Ave. A
212.979.9595

East Village (cont'd)

Patricia Adams
115 St. Mark's Pl.
212.420.0077

Flatiron

Club Monaco
21st St. (@ 5th Ave.)
212.352.0936

NoHo

Nylon Squid
222 Lafayette St.
212.334.6554

NoLIta

Asp
185 Mulberry St.
646.621.3524

NoLIta (cont'd)

Baby Blue Line
238 Mott St.
212.226.5866

Christine Ganeaux
45 Crosby St.
212.431.4462

Claire Blaydon
202A Mott St.
212.219.1490

Inhumane Shop
195 Mulberry St.
212.331.0499

Kinnu
43 Spring St.
212.334.4775

Minlee
7 Prince St.
212.334.6978

Only Hearts
230 Mott St.
212.431.3694

Product
219 Mott St.
212.219.2224

NoLIta (cont'd)

Red Wong
181 Mulberry St.
212.625.1638

X-Large
267 Lafayette St.
212.334.4480

SoHo

Afterlife
9 Greene St.
212.625.3167

Agnis B.
9 Greene St.
212.741.2585

Agnis B.
116-118 Prince St.
212.925.4649

Anne Fontaine
93 Greene St.
212.373.3154
www.annefontaine.com

SoHo (cont'd)

A.P.C.
131 Mercer St.
212.966.9685

Baby Phat
129 Prince St.
212.533.7428

Betsey Johnson
138 Wooster St.
212.995.5048

CD Shades
154 Spring St.

Club Monaco
Prince St.
646.533.8930

FCUK
435 W. Broadway

Haneza
93 Grand St.
212.343.9373

Harriet Love
126 Prince St.
212.966.2280

SoHo (cont'd)

Hugo Boss
132 Greene St.
212.965.1300

Ina
21 Prince St.
212.334.9048

Ina
101 Thompson St.
212.941.4757

Joseph
106 Greene St.
212.343.7071

Kirna Zabete
96 Greene St.
212.941.9656

Kors Michael Kors
159 Mercer St.

Lucky Brand Jeans
38 Greene St.
212.625.0707

Mare
426 W. Broadway
212.343.1110

SoHo (cont'd)

Miu Miu
100 Prince St.
212.334.5156

Nicole Miller
134 Prince St.
212.343.1362

Nuovo Melodrom
60 Greene St.
212.219.0013
www.nuovomelodrom.com

Olive Bette's
158 Spring St.
646.613.8772

Onward
172 Mercer St.
212.274.1255

Pleats Please by Issey Miyake
128 Wooster St-212.226.360
soho@pleats-please.com

Plein Sud
70 Greene St.

Product
71 Mercer St.
212.625.1630

SoHo (cont'd)

Quicksilver
109-111 Spring St.
212.334.4500

R by 45 rpm
169 Mercer St.
917.237.0045

Rampage
127 Prince St.
917.995.9569

Replay
109 Prince St.
212.673.6300

Rugby North America
115 Mercer St.
212.431.3069

Shabby Chic
93 Wooster St.
212.274.9842

Shin Choi
119 Mercer St.
212.625.9202

Sisley
159 W. Broadway
212.375.0538

SoHo (cont'd)

Stussy NYC
140 Wooster St.
212.995.8787

Tardini
142 Wooster St.
212.253.7692

Tehen
91 Greene St.
212.925.4788

Tocca
161 Mercer St.
212.343.3912

Togs SoHo
68 Spring St.
917.237.1882

Ventilo
69 Greene St.
212.625.3660

Vivienne Tam
99 Greene St.
212.966.2398

Wolford Boutique
122 Greene St.
212.343.0808

SoHo (cont'd)

Yohji Yamamoto USA
103 Grand St.
212.966.9066

TriBeCa

Assets London
152 Franklin St.
212.219.8777

Detour
425-475 W. Broadway
212.625.1820

Seam
117 W. Broadway
212.732.9411

Union Square

Emporio Armani
110 5th Ave.
212.727.3240

Union Square (cont'd)

Paul Smith
108 5th Ave. (@ 16th)
212.627.9770

Variazioni
104 5th Ave.

Zara
101 5th Ave. (@ 17th)
212.741.0555

Upper East Side

Agnis B.
1063 Madison Ave.
212.570.9333

BCBG Max Mara
813 Madison Ave.
212.879.6100

Barney's New York
Madison Ave. at 61st St.
212.826.8900

Upper East Side (cont'd)

Bebe
1044 Madison Ave.
212.517.2323

Bebe
1127 3rd Ave.
212.935.2444

Bergdorf Goodman
754 5th Ave. (@58th St.)
212.753.7300

Betsey Johnson
1060 Madison Ave.
212.734.1257

Bloomingdale's
1000 3rd Ave. (59th/60th)
212.705.2000

Bottega Veneta
655 Madison Ave
212.371.5511

Burberry London
9 E. 57th St. (Madison/5th)
212.371.5010

Upper East Side (cont'd)

Calypso
935 Madison Ave.
212.535.4100

Celine
667 Madison Ave.
212.486.9700

Cerruti
789 Madison Ave.
212.327.2222

Club Monaco
65th St. (@ 3rd Ave.)
646.533.8930

DKNY
655 Madison Ave. (@60th St.)
212.223.3569

Emporio Armani
601 Madison Ave.
212.317.0800

Ensoie
988 Madison Ave.
212.717.7958

Upper East Side (cont'd)

Episode
625 Madison Ave.
212.755.6061

Eres
621 Madison Ave.
212.223.3550

Fogal
680 Madison Ave. (@ 61st)
212.355.3254
info@fogal.com

Genny
831 Madison Ave.
212.249.9660

Gia Franco Ferre
845 Madison Ave.
212.717.5430

Gianni Versace
815 Madison Ave.
212.744.6868

Gucci
685 5th Ave. (@54th)
212.826.2600

Upper East Side (cont'd)

Issey Miyake
992 Madison Ave.
212.439.7822
madison@isseymiyake.com

Joseph
796 Madison Ave
212.327.1773

Joseph
804 Madison Ave
212.570.0077

Krizia
769 Madison Ave
212.879.1211

Loro Piana
821 Madison Ave.

Michael Kors
974 Madison Ave.
212.452.4685

Moga
715 Madison Ave.
212.751.7506

Women's Clothes

Upper East Side (cont'd)

Moschino
303 Madison Ave.
212.639.9600

Olive Bette's
1070 Madison Ave.
212.717.9566

Robert Marc
782 Madison Ave.
212.737.6000

Robert Marc
1046 Madison Ave.
212.988.9600

Robert Marc
1300 Madison Ave.
212.722.1600

Roberto Cavalli
711 Madison Ave.

Sonia Rykiel
849 Madison Ave.
212.396.3060

Super Runners Shop
1246 3rd Ave.
212.249.2133

Upper East Side (cont'd)

Super Runners Shop
1337 Lexington Ave.
212.369.6010

Tse
827 Madison Ave.
212.472.7790

Valentino
747 Madison Ave.
212.772.6969

Versace
815 Madison Ave.
212.744.6868

Vertigo
755 Madison Ave.
212.439.9826

Wolford
619 Madison Ave. (@ 77th)
212.688.4850

Worldly Things
837 Madison Ave.
212.988.7810

Upper East Side (cont'd)

Yves Saint Laurent
855 Madison Ave.
212.988.3821

Zara
750 Lexington Ave. (@ 59th)
212.754.1120

Upper West Side

Assets London
464 Columbus Ave.
212.874.8253

Bath Island
469 Amsterdam Ave.
212.787.9415
bathisland@netscape.net
www.bathisland.com

Betsey Johnson
24 Columbus Ave.

Upper West Side (cont'd)

Capry Uomo
105 W. 72nd St.
212.724.7500

CD Shades
300 Columbus Ave.

Club Monaco
2376 Broadway
212.579.2587

Darryl's
490-492 Amsterdam Ave.
(83rd/84th)
212.874.6677
212.721.2709

FCUK
1270 6th Ave.

FCUK
700 Broadway

FCUK
304 Columbus Ave.

Frank Stella Clothiers
440 Columbus Ave. (@ 81st)
646.877.5566

Upper West Side (cont'd)

Granny Made
381 Amsterdam Ave.
(78th/79th)
212.496.1222
www.granny-made.com

Laina Jane Lingerie
416 Amsterdam Ave.
212.727.7032

Laura Ashley, Inc.
398 Columbus Ave.
212.496.5110

Liana
324 Columbus Ave.
(75th/76th)
212.873.8746

Montmartre
2212 Broadway
212.875.8430

Montmartre
247 Columbus Ave.
212.721.7760

Off Broadway Boutique
139 W. 72nd St.
212.724.6713

Upper West Side (cont'd)

Olive Bette's
252 Columbus Ave (@ 72nd)
212.579.2178

Really Great Things
284A Columbus Ave.
212.787.5354

Sisley
2308 Broadway
212.769.0121

Super Runners Shop
360 Amsterdam Ave.
212.787.7665

Tibet Bazaar
473 Amsterdam Ave.
(82nd/83rd)
212.595.8487

Zan Boutique
2394 Broadway
212.877.4853

Zara
34th St - 39th St.
(@ 5th Ave.)
212.868.6551

West 23rd - 59th St.

Frank Stella Clothiers
921 7th Ave. (@ 58th St.)
646.957.1600

Hermes
11 E. 57th St. (6th/7th)
212.751.3181

Zan Boutique
1666 Broadway (51st/52nd)
212.582.5580

West Village

Arleen Bowman
353 Bleecker St.
212.645.8740

Laina Jane Lingerie
35 Christopher St.
212.727.7032

London Boutique
85 Christopher St.
212.647.9106

West Village (cont'd)

Sleek on Bleecker
361 Bleecker St.
212.243.0284
sleek@att.net

Yamak, Inc.
321 1/2 Bleecker St.
(Christopher/Grove)
212.807.9100

All Areas

Mail Boxes, Etc.
All Locations

Chelsea

A.I. Friedman
44 W. 18th St.
212.243.9000
www.aifriedman.com

East 23rd - 59th St.

Davidoff
35 Madison Ave
212.751.9060
800.548.4623

Paper Emporium
35A 2nd Ave
212.697.6573

East 23rd - 59th St. (cont'd)

Rebecca Moss, LTD
510 Madison Ave
212.832.7671

Scully & Scully Park Ave.
504 Park Ave. (@59th)
800.223.3717

East Village

Downtown Yarn
45 Ave. A
212.995.5991

Flatiron

Typogram
318 W. 39th St.

212.736.3686

NoLIta

French General
35 Crosby St.
(Broome/Grand)
212.343.7474

SoHo

Typogram
71 Spring St.
212.219.9770

Upper East Side

Sharper Image
900 Madison Ave.

West Village

Condomania
351 Bleecker St.
212.691.9442

West Village (cont'd)

Enfluerage
321 Bleecker St.
212.691.1610

Flightool
96 Greenwich Ave.
212.691.0001